HOW TO DRAW ANIMALS FOR KIDS

Easy Step-by-Step Guide

WIZZARTO

Contents

Introduction

Ready to draw cute animals?
Looking for a way to take your drawing
in a new direction? Interested in trying
something new?

This guide is for anyone who wants to
learn to draw cute animals, from kids
to adults, no matter their experience
level. The guide features an easy-to-follow 8-step
process for each animal that anyone can practice
following for amazing drawings.

Recommended Supplies

Here are some basic tools and
materials you will need before
starting:

Pencil, eraser, pencil
sharpener

How to Use This Book!

Make sure to carefully follow each step in the drawing diagram and remember to remove any unnecessary lines as you go along.

The grid copy method

The grid copy method helps you draw a picture easily by breaking it down into smaller boxes.

You start with box A1 and work your way down to box J10.

Have fun!

Just focus on the details in the box you're working on and try to draw them as accurately as you can.

Start here!

focus on one box at a time!

After you have completed your drawing, you can add your own creative touches or add color to make it even more special and unique!

Drawing Tips

Look at All the Steps First
Looking at all 8 steps before you start will help you draw the animal big enough to practice and develop your sense of how the drawing will go.

Draw Lightly
When you're drawing, do it lightly with a pencil at first. Then, you can come back with colors or a pen once the animal looks the way you want.

Don't Worry About Perfection
No two artists will draw the same animal, and that's great! Your drawing doesn't need to look exactly like the example since it reflects your style.

Practice Each Animal
No one draws something perfectly the first time. Therefore, you may need to practice the animals several times so that they look how you want.

Have fun
Drawing is a fun experience, and you should enjoy making these animals. Don't be afraid to do crazy patterns or unusual colors too!

Learn a Little
Each animal's page has interesting facts about the animal. The book combines drawing and learning into one fun experience.

"Bring your favorite animals to life with 'How to Draw Animals for Kids'. Get ready to unleash your creativity —grab your pencils and let's begin!"

Alpaca

START!

1

2

3

4

5

6

7

8

Alpacas have good memories and can remember their friends for years.

A B C D E F G H I J

1
2
3
4
5
6
7
8
9
10

A B C D E F G H I J

1
2
3
4
5
6
7
8
9
10

Anglerfish

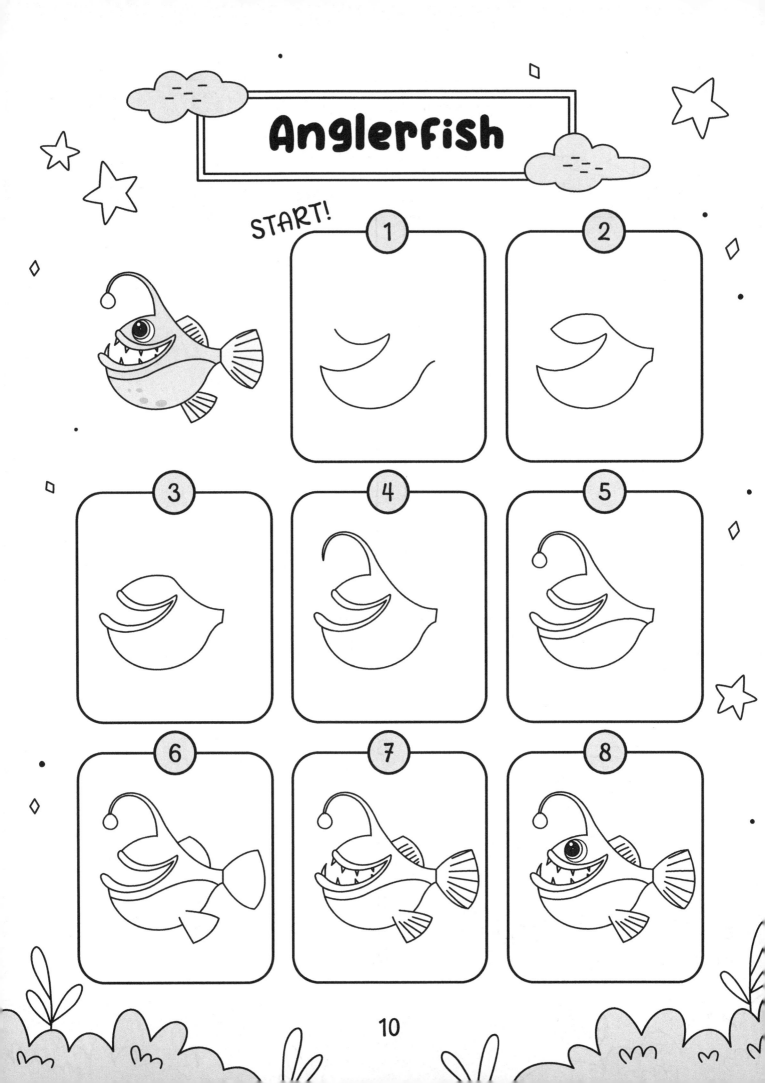

START!

1 2 3 4 5 6 7 8

10

They live deep in the ocean, up to a mile down!

Practice Here

A B C D E F G H I J

1
2
3
4
5
6
7
8
9
10

A B C D E F G H I J

1
2
3
4
5
6
7
8
9
10

11

Ant

START!

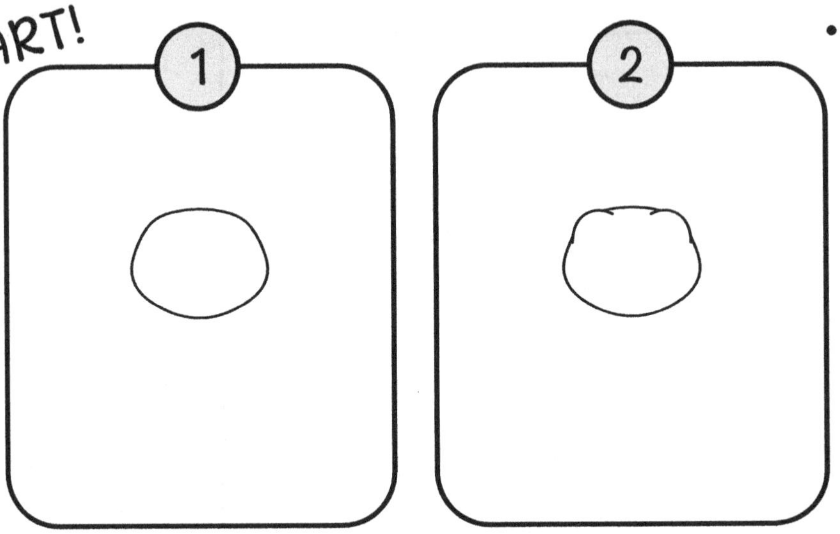

1

2

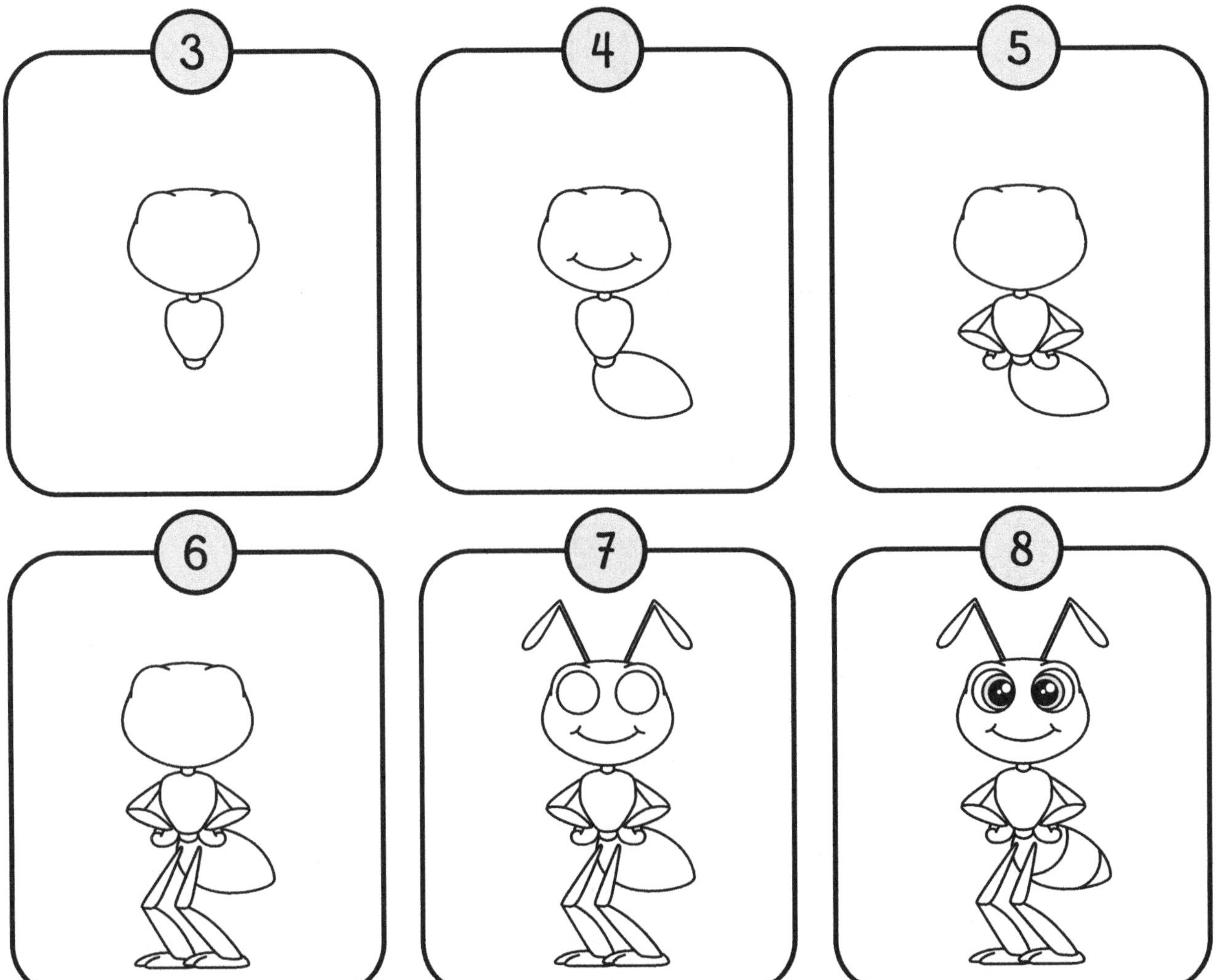

3

4

5

6

7

8

12

Ants leave scent trails so that they don't get lost going home.

Practice Here

A B C D E F G H I J

1
2
3
4
5
6
7
8
9
10

A B C D E F G H I J

1
2
3
4
5
6
7
8
9
10

Axolotl

START!

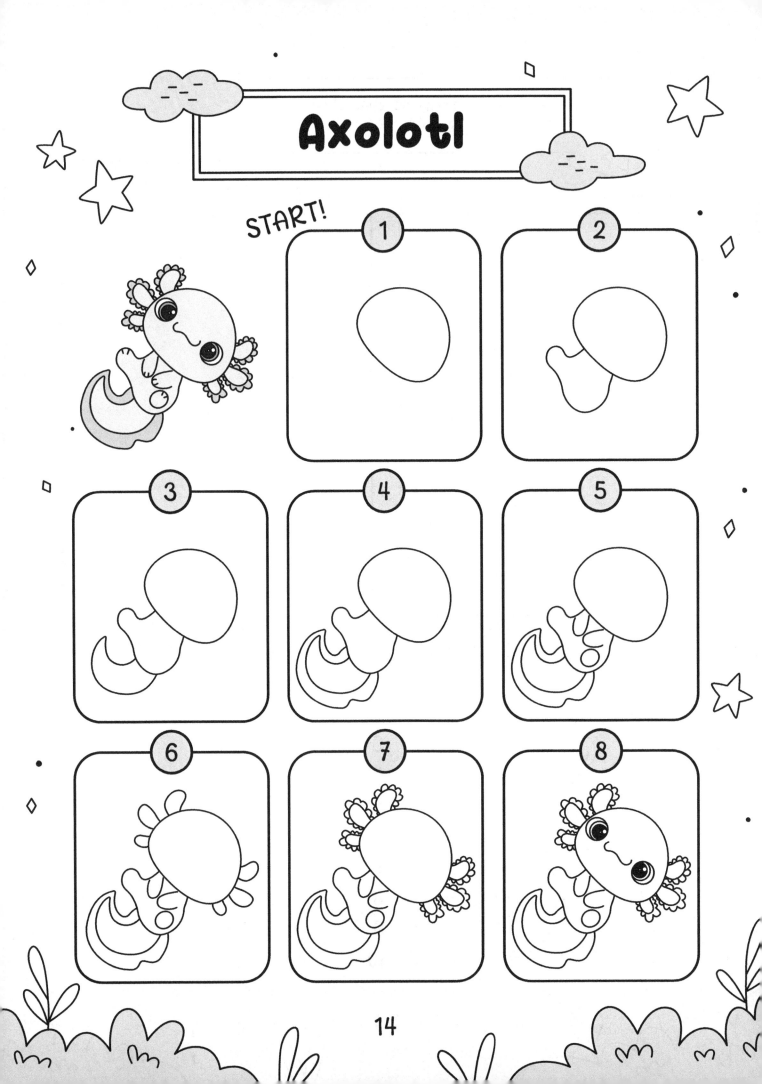

They have a superpower – they can regrow lost body parts, including their hearts.

Practice Here

A B C D E F G H I J

1
2
3
4
5
6
7
8
9
10

A B C D E F G H I J

1
2
3
4
5
6
7
8
9
10

Bat

START!

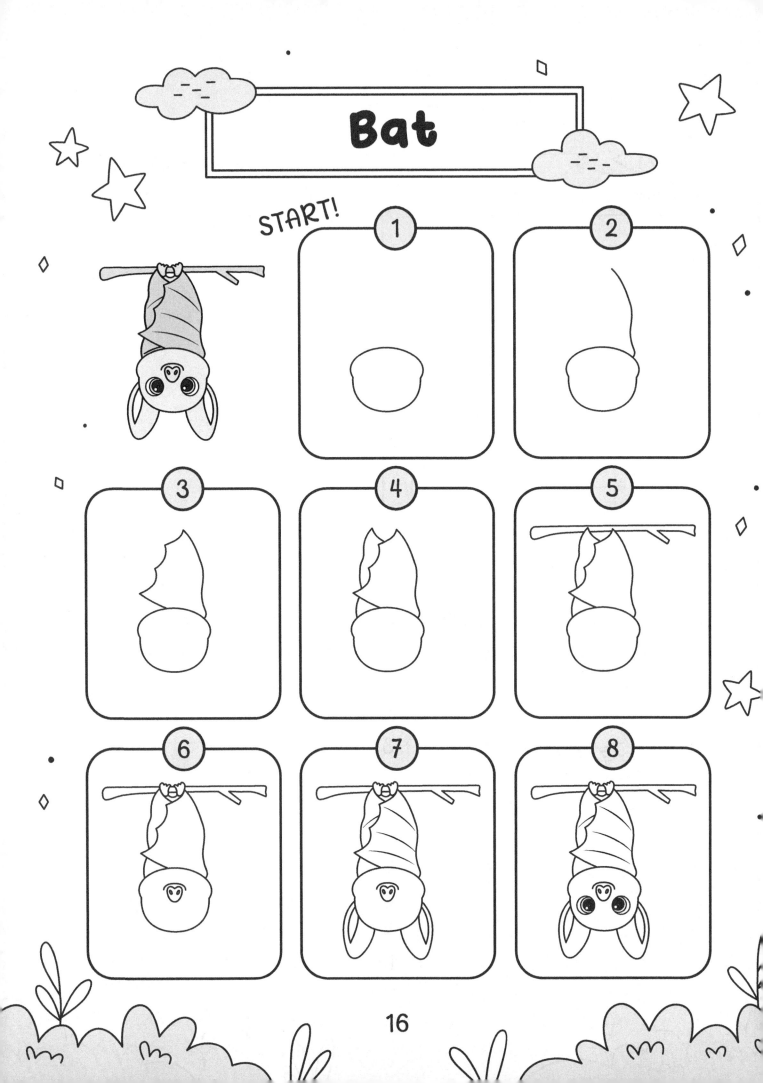

Bats hang upside down because it's the
best position for quick takeoff.

Practice Here

A B C D E F G H I J   A B C D E F G H I J

1   1
2   2
3   3
4   4
5   5
6   6
7   7
8   8
9   9
10   10

Beaver

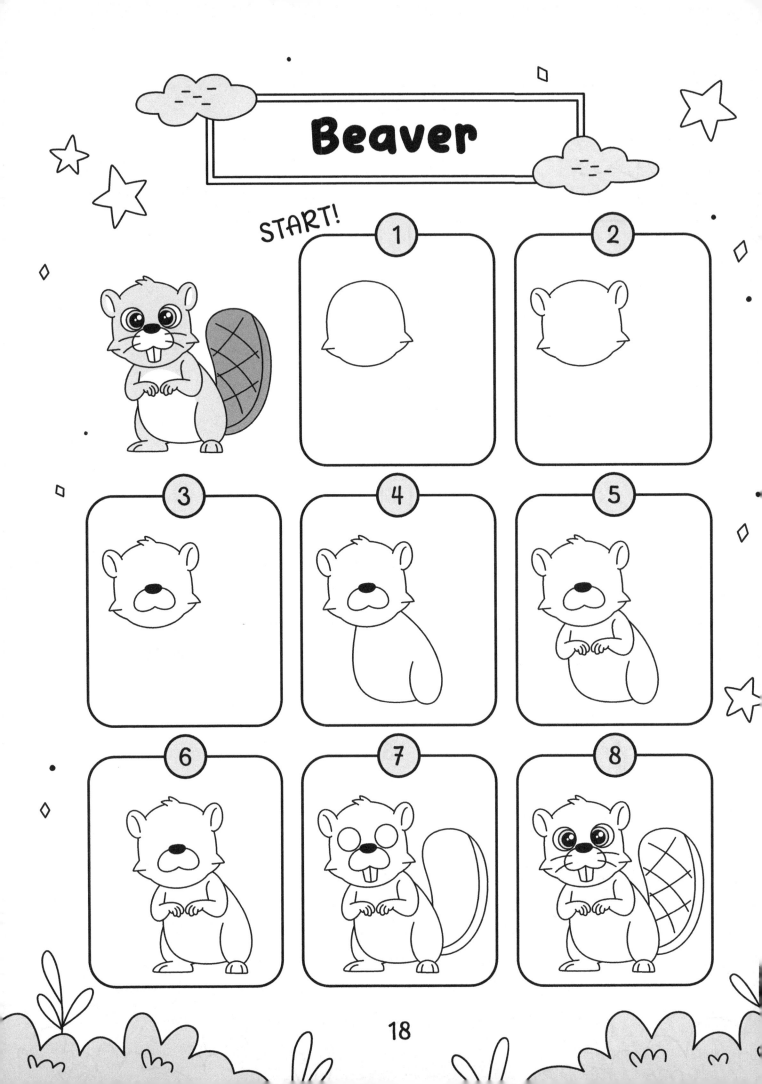

START!

1
2
3
4
5
6
7
8

Beavers can stay underwater for up to 15 minutes without breathing.

Practice Here

A B C D E F G H I J

1
2
3
4
5
6
7
8
9
10

A B C D E F G H I J

1
2
3
4
5
6
7
8
9
10

Bee

START!

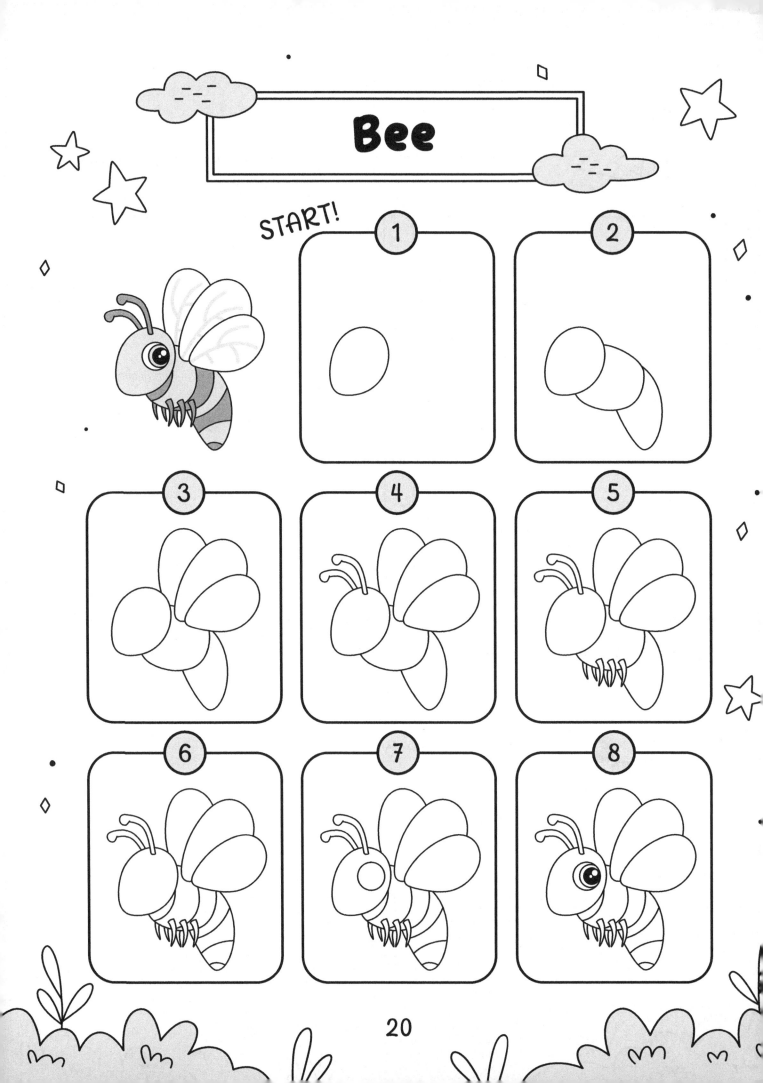

20

Bees can recognize human faces, just like we recognize them.

Practice Here

A B C D E F G H I J

1
2
3
4
5
6
7
8
9
10

A B C D E F G H I J

1
2
3
4
5
6
7
8
9
10

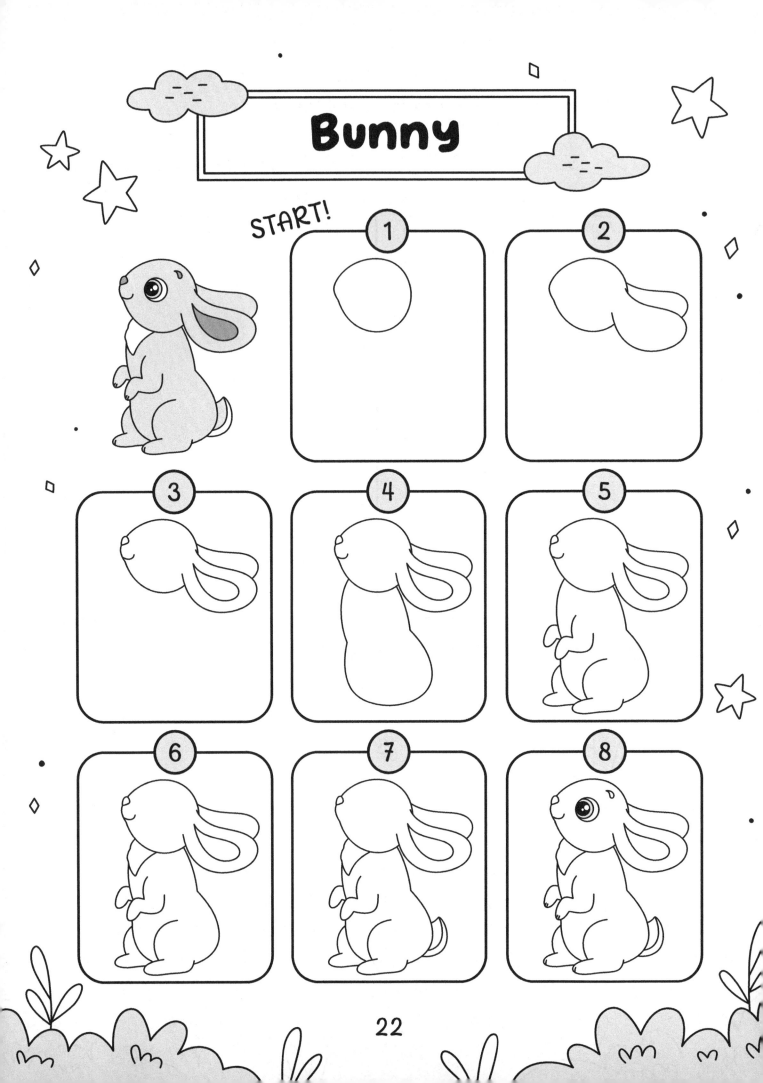

Bunny

START!

1

2

3

4

5

6

7

8

22

They can sleep with their eyes open.

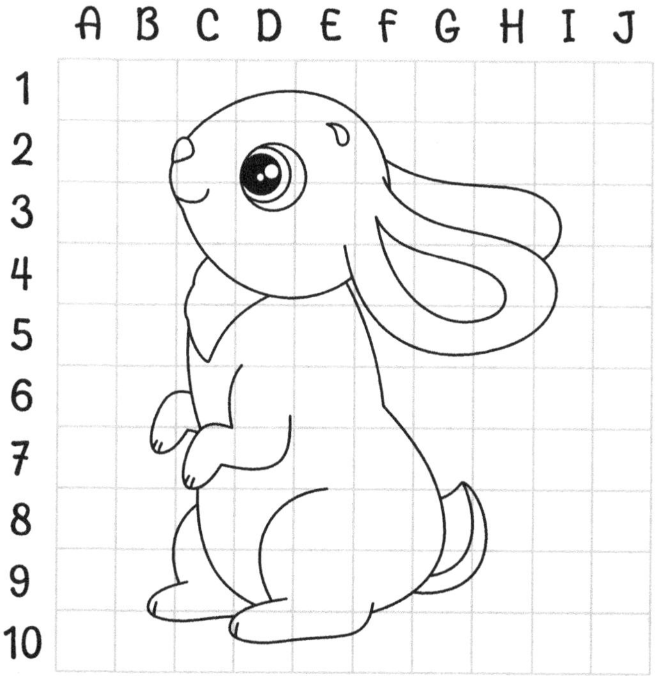

A B C D E F G H I J

1
2
3
4
5
6
7
8
9
10

A B C D E F G H I J

1
2
3
4
5
6
7
8
9
10

Cat

START!

They can make over 100 different sounds.

Practice Here

A B C D E F G H I J

1
2
3
4
5
6
7
8
9
10

A B C D E F G H I J

1
2
3
4
5
6
7
8
9
10

25

Crab

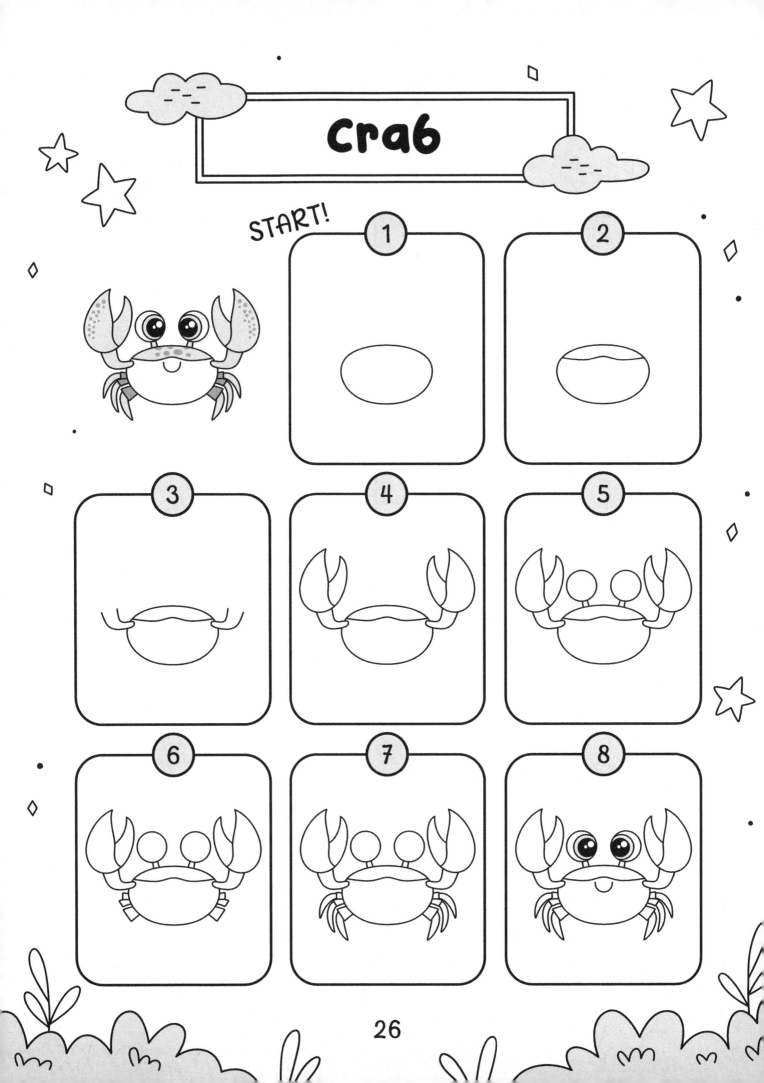

START!

1

2

3

4

5

6

7

8

26

Crabs use their pincers for fighting and feeding.

Practice Here

A B C D E F G H I J

1
2
3
4
5
6
7
8
9
10

A B C D E F G H I J

1
2
3
4
5
6
7
8
9
10

Crocodile

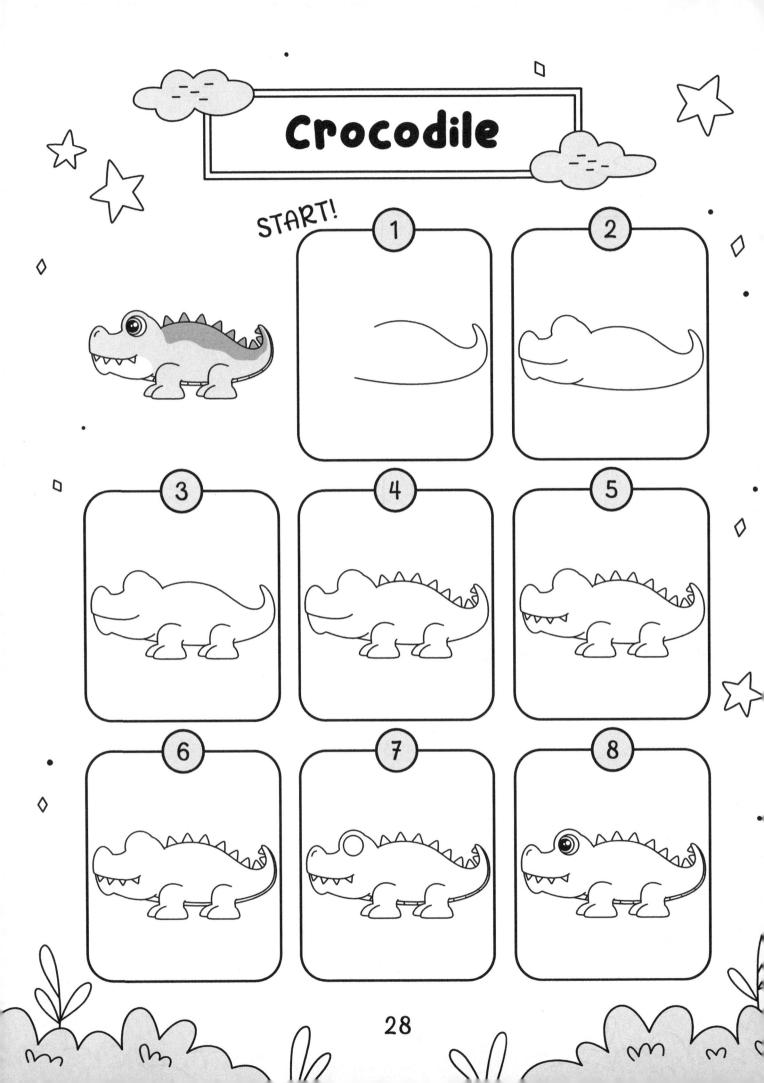

START!

1
2
3
4
5
6
7
8

Crocodiles can't stick out their tongues.

Practice Here

A B C D E F G H I J

1
2
3
4
5
6
7
8
9
10

A B C D E F G H I J

1
2
3
4
5
6
7
8
9
10

Deer

START!

There are over 60 different species of deer.

A B C D E F G H I J

1
2
3
4
5
6
7
8
9
10

A B C D E F G H I J

1
2
3
4
5
6
7
8
9
10

Diplodocus

START!

1

2

3

4

5

6

7

8

Diplodocus was one of the longest dinosaurs, reaching up to 90 feet!

A B C D E F G H I J

1
2
3
4
5
6
7
8
9
10

A B C D E F G H I J

1
2
3
4
5
6
7
8
9
10

33

Dog

START!

Dogs' whiskers help them "see" in the dark.

Practice Here

A B C D E F G H I J

	A	B	C	D	E	F	G	H	I	J
1										
2										
3										
4										
5										
6										
7										
8										
9										
10										

A B C D E F G H I J

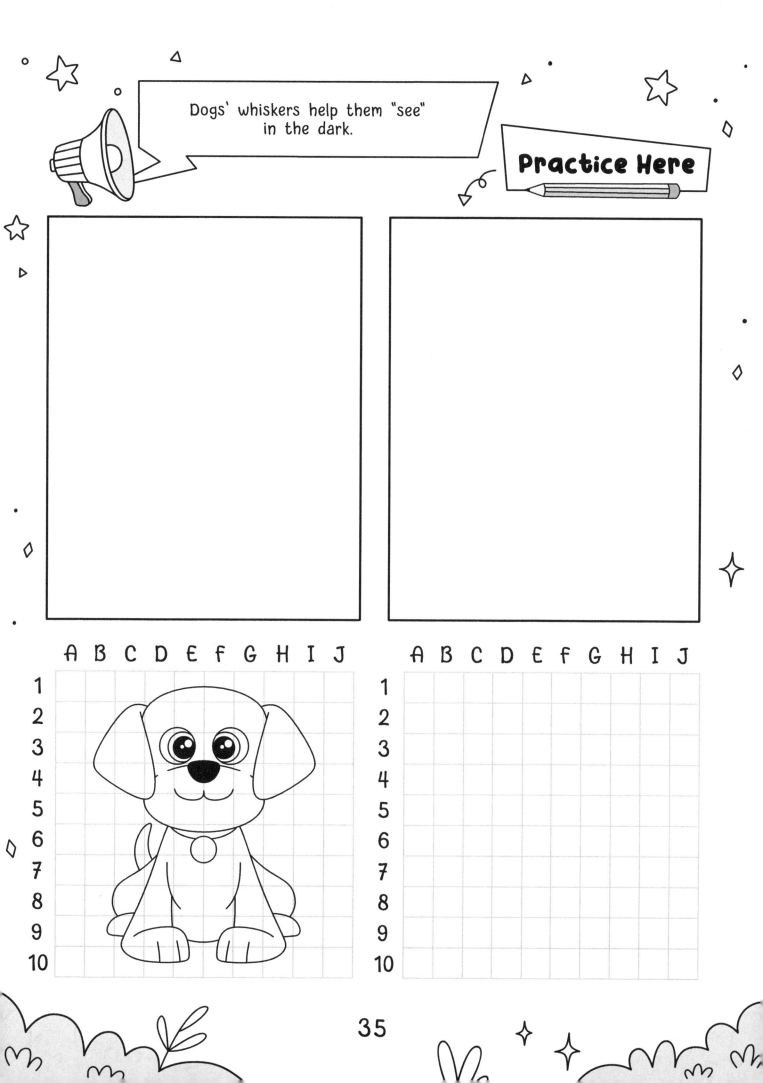

Fennec

START!

1
2
3
4
5
6
7
8

The soles of a fennec's feet are protected from hot sand by thick fur.

Practice Here

A B C D E F G H I J

1
2
3
4
5
6
7
8
9
10

A B C D E F G H I J

1
2
3
4
5
6
7
8
9
10

Flamingo

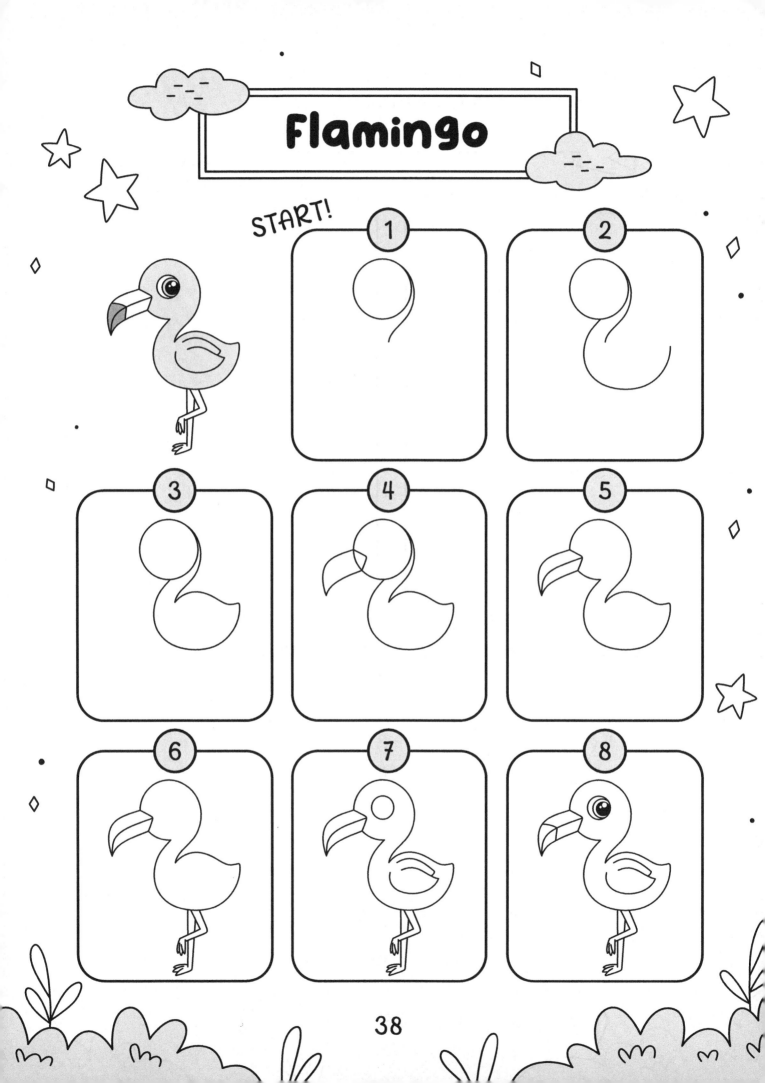

START!

1 2 3 4 5 6 7 8

38

Baby flamingos are born grey and white, not pink.

Practice Here

A B C D E F G H I J

1
2
3
4
5
6
7
8
9
10

A B C D E F G H I J

1
2
3
4
5
6
7
8
9
10

Fox

START!

40

Some foxes can climb trees.

Practice Here

A B C D E F G H I J

1
2
3
4
5
6
7
8
9
10

A B C D E F G H I J

1
2
3
4
5
6
7
8
9
10

Frog

START!

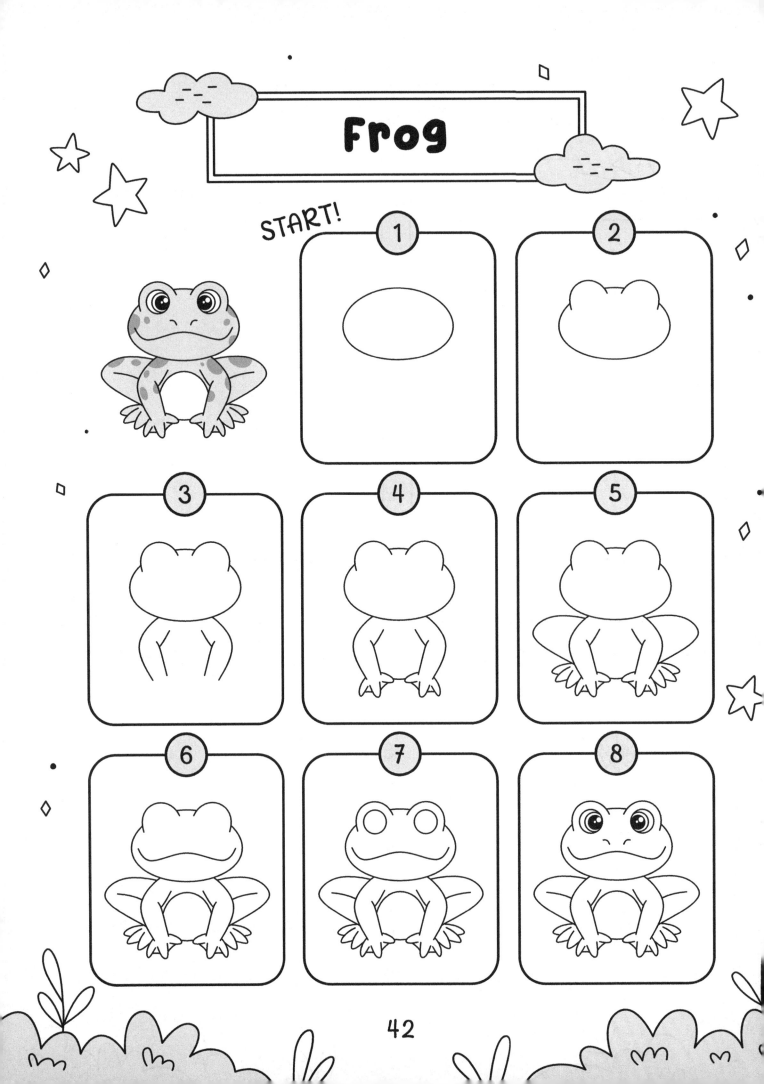

frogs absorb water through their skin,
they don't need to drink.

Practice Here

A B C D E F G H I J

1
2
3
4
5
6
7
8
9
10

A B C D E F G H I J

1
2
3
4
5
6
7
8
9
10

43

Gecko

START!

Geckos have "sticky" feet that allow them to walk on ceilings.

Practice Here

A B C D E F G H I J

1
2
3
4
5
6
7
8
9
10

A B C D E F G H I J

1
2
3
4
5
6
7
8
9
10

Giraffe

START!

They only sleep for about
30 minutes a day.

Practice Here

	A	B	C	D	E	F	G	H	I	J
1										
2										
3										
4										
5										
6										
7										
8										
9										
10										

Hermit Crab

START!

1

2

3

4

5

6

7

8

48

They have ten legs but use only six for walking.

A B C D E F G H I J

1
2
3
4
5
6
7
8
9
10

A B C D E F G H I J

1
2
3
4
5
6
7
8
9
10

49

Hippo

START!

Hippos spend most of their day in water to keep cool.

Practice Here

A B C D E F G H I J

1
2
3
4
5
6
7
8
9
10

A B C D E F G H I J

1
2
3
4
5
6
7
8
9
10

Horse

START!

Horses can sleep both standing up and lying down.

Practice Here

	A	B	C	D	E	F	G	H	I	J
1										
2										
3										
4										
5										
6										
7										
8										
9										
10										

Jellyfish

START!

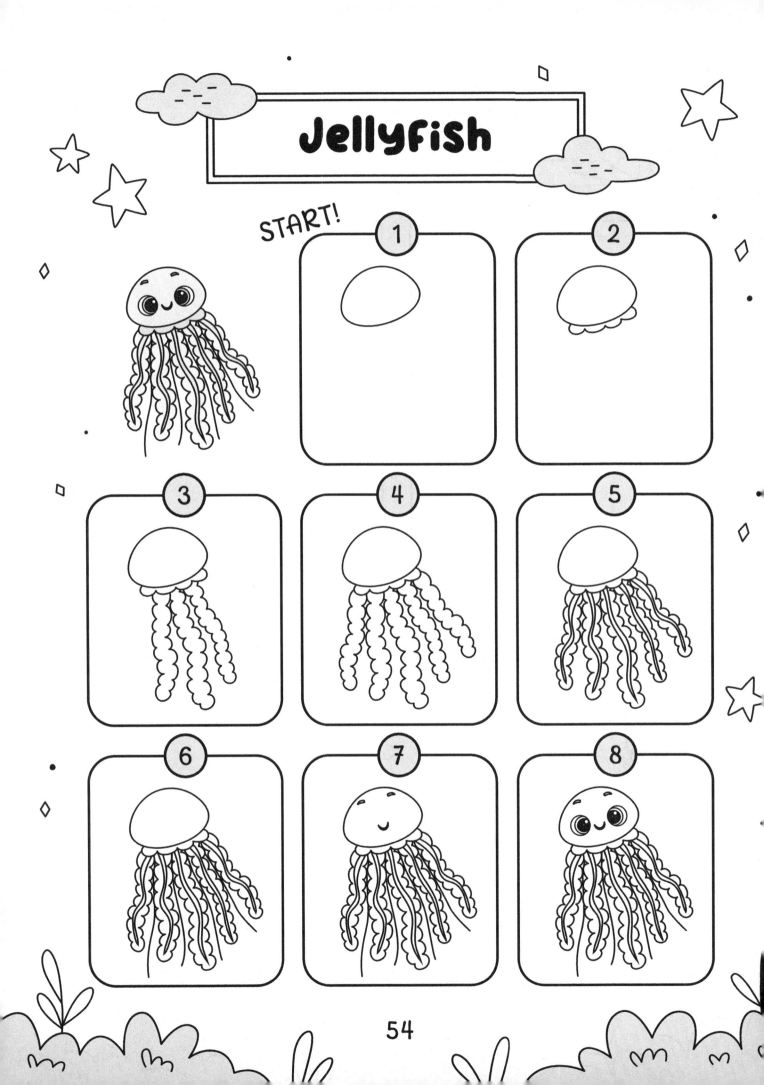

1 **2** **3** **4** **5** **6** **7** **8**

54

Some types of jellyfish can glow
in the dark.

Practice Here

A B C D E F G H I J

1
2
3
4
5
6
7
8
9
10

A B C D E F G H I J

1
2
3
4
5
6
7
8
9
10

koala

START!

Koalas have a pouch where the joey grows and develops.

Practice Here

A B C D E F G H I J

1
2
3
4
5
6
7
8
9
10

A B C D E F G H I J

1
2
3
4
5
6
7
8
9
10

Lemur

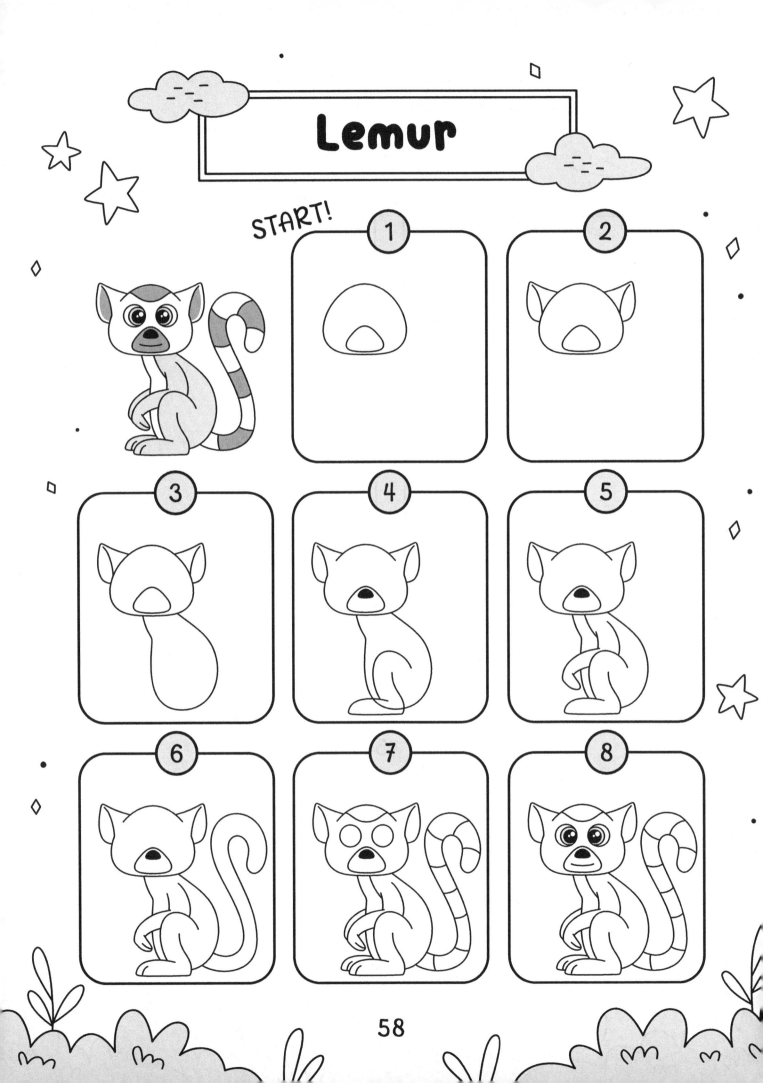

START!

1
2
3
4
5
6
7
8

They have large, round reflective eyes to help them see at night.

Practice Here

A B C D E F G H I J

| | 1 | 2 | 3 | 4 | 5 | 6 | 7 | 8 | 9 | 10 |

A B C D E F G H I J

| | 1 | 2 | 3 | 4 | 5 | 6 | 7 | 8 | 9 | 10 |

Leopard

START!

1
2
3
4
5
6
7
8

60

Leopards are skilled climbers and often store their food in trees.

Practice Here

A B C D E F G H I J

1
2
3
4
5
6
7
8
9
10

A B C D E F G H I J

1
2
3
4
5
6
7
8
9
10

Lion

START!

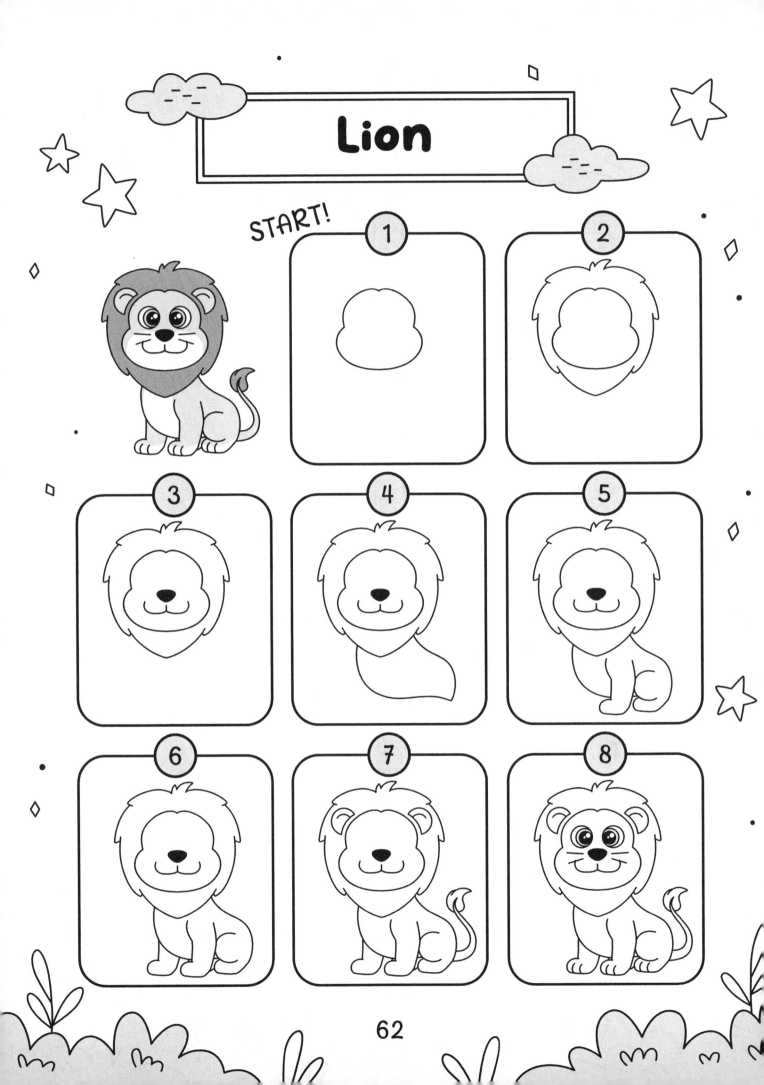

Lions cannot roar until they are 2 years old.

Practice Here

A B C D E F G H I J

1
2
3
4
5
6
7
8
9
10

A B C D E F G H I J

1
2
3
4
5
6
7
8
9
10

Monkey

START!

1
2
3
4
5
6
7
8

Monkeys can make over 30 facial expressions, just like humans.

Practice Here

A B C D E F G H I J

1
2
3
4
5
6
7
8
9
10

A B C D E F G H I J

1
2
3
4
5
6
7
8
9
10

Moorish Idol

START!

Practice Here

A B C D E F G H I J

1
2
3
4
5
6
7
8
9
10

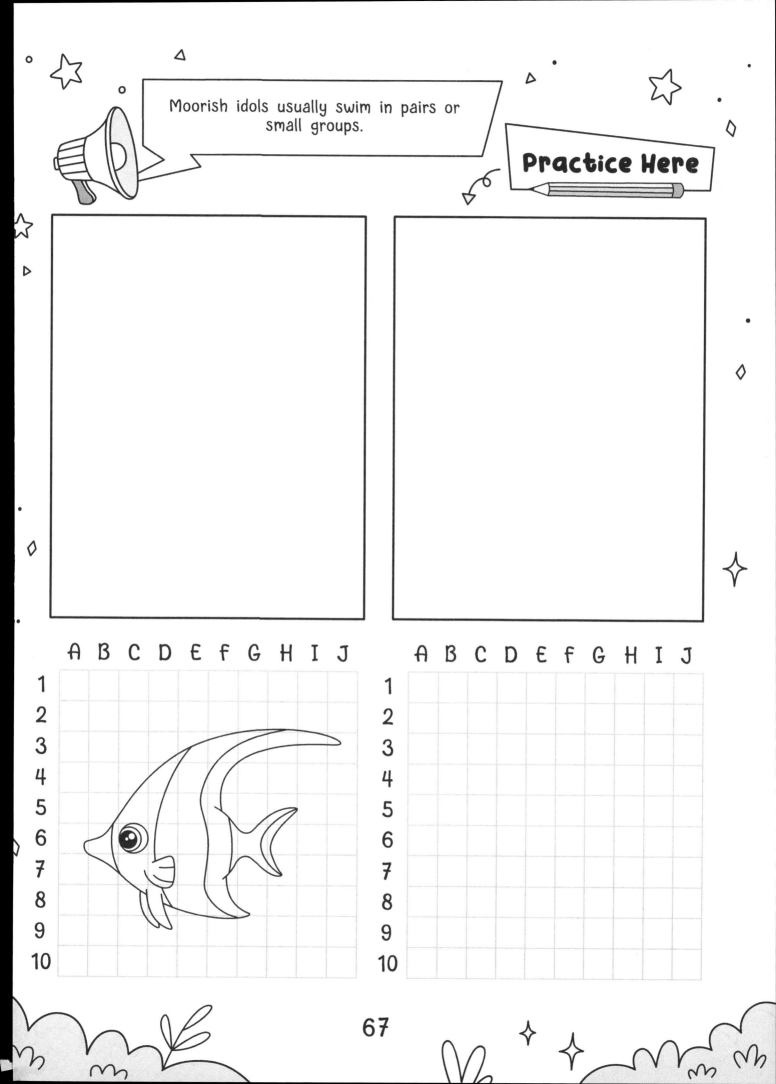

A B C D E F G H I J

1
2
3
4
5
6
7
8
9
10

Mosquoito

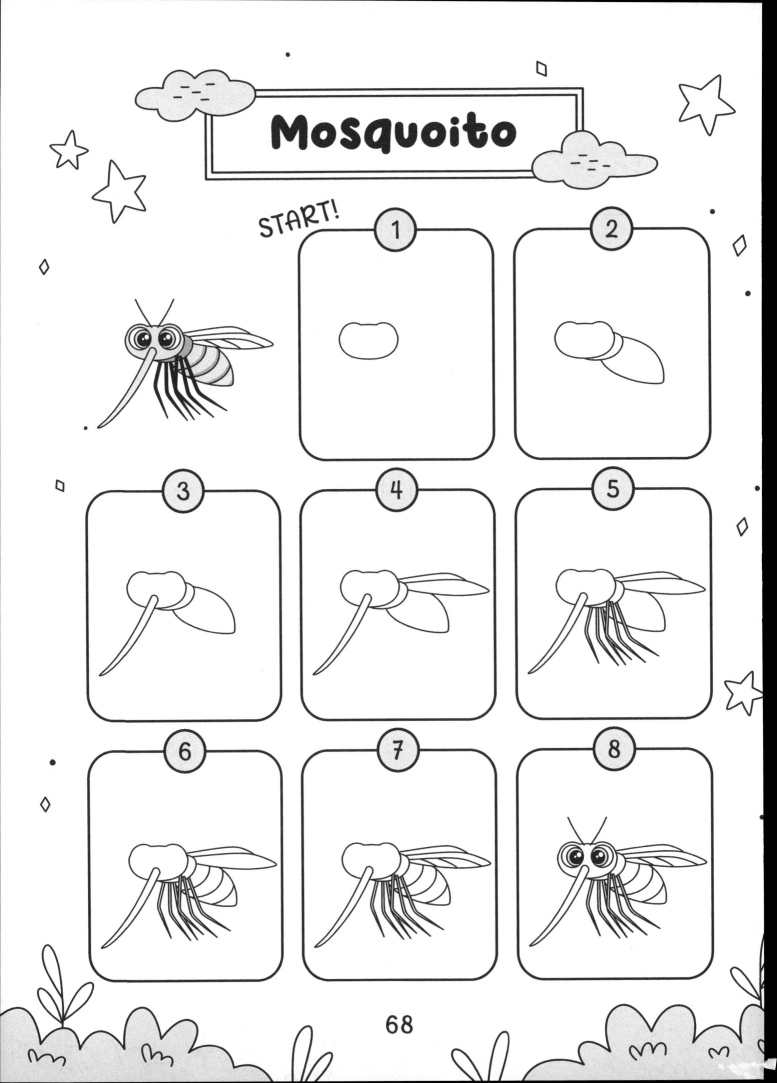

START!

1

2

3

4

5

6

7

8

Only female mosquitoes bite because they need blood to lay eggs.

Practice Here

A B C D E F G H I J

1
2
3
4
5
6
7
8
9
10

A B C D E F G H I J

1
2
3
4
5
6
7
8
9
10

Mouse

START!

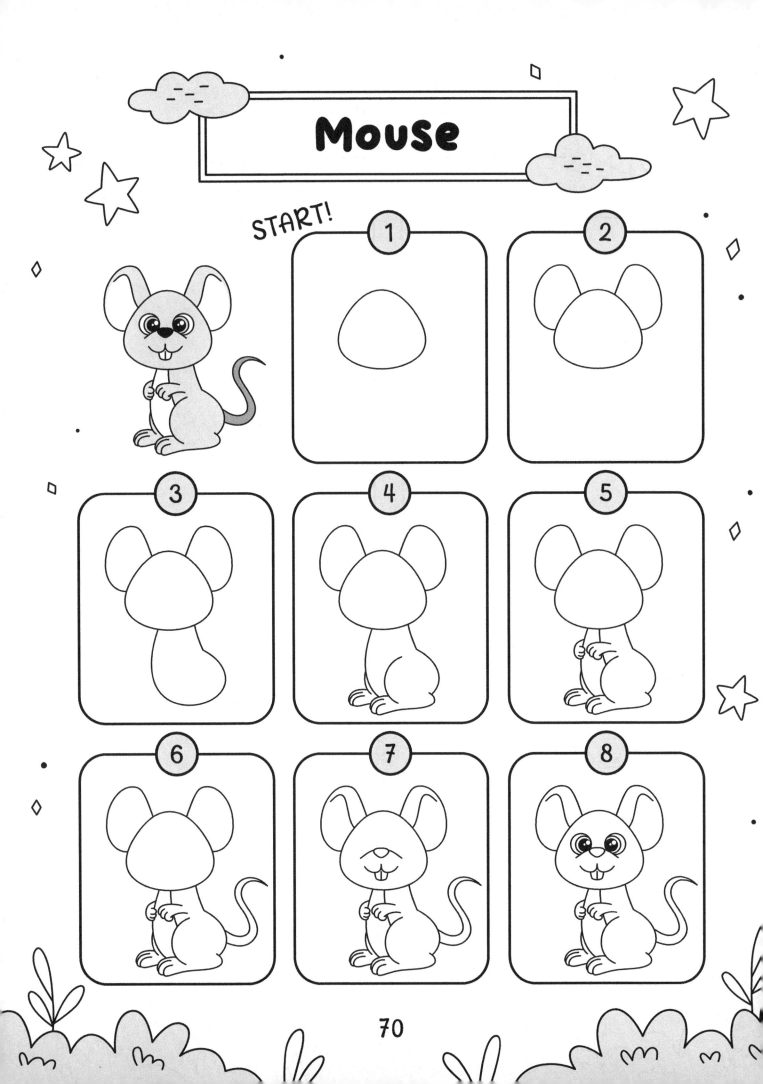

70

A mouse can squeeze through holes as small as a pencil!

Practice Here

A B C D E F G H I J

1
2
3
4
5
6
7
8
9
10

A B C D E F G H I J

1
2
3
4
5
6
7
8
9
10

Narwhal

START!

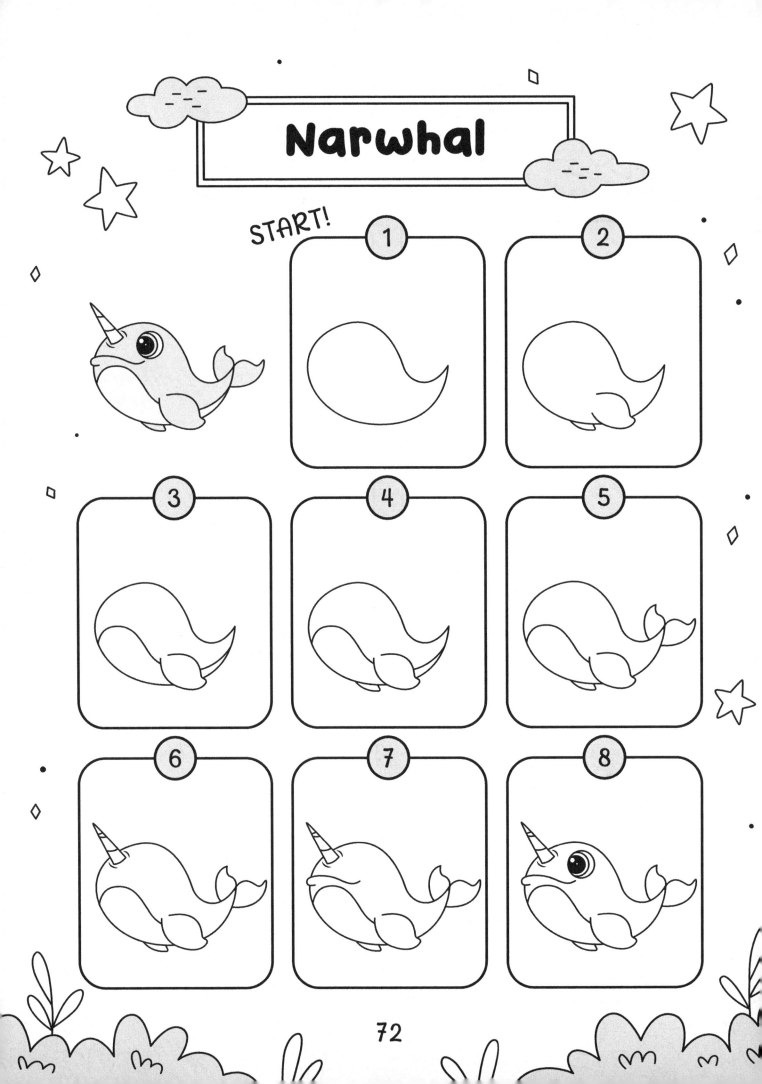

Narwhals change color with age.

Practice Here

A B C D E F G H I J

1
2
3
4
5
6
7
8
9
10

A B C D E F G H I J

1
2
3
4
5
6
7
8
9
10

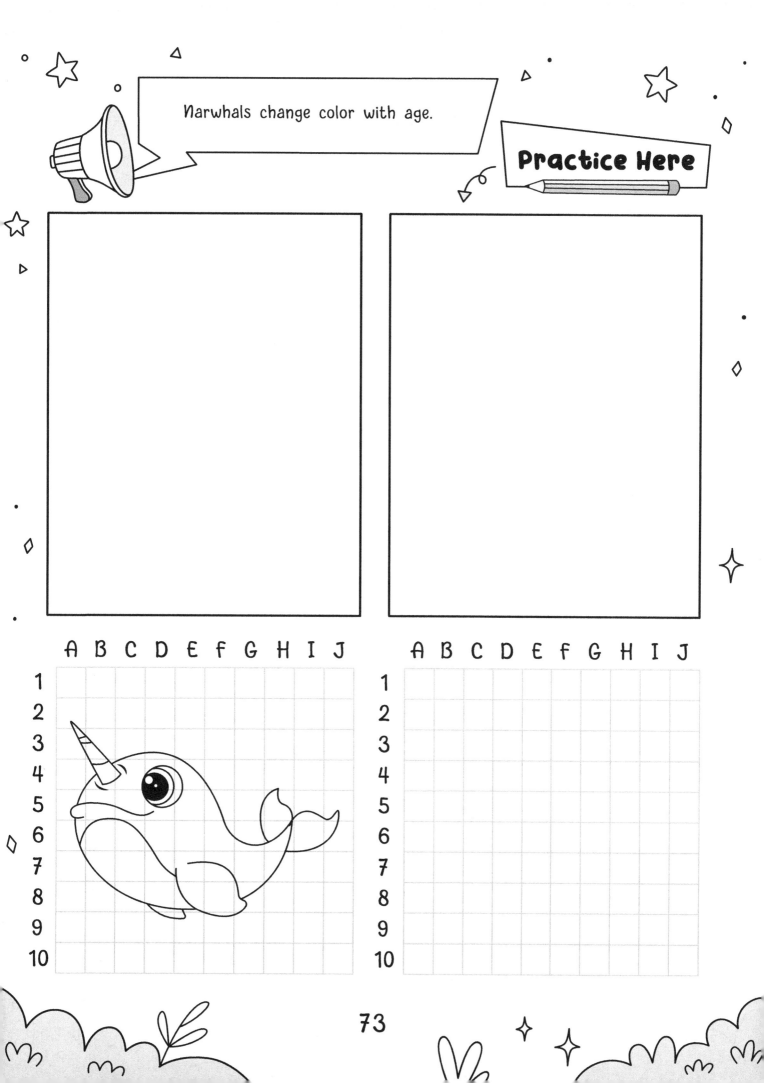

Octopus

START!

1

2

3

4

5

6

7

8

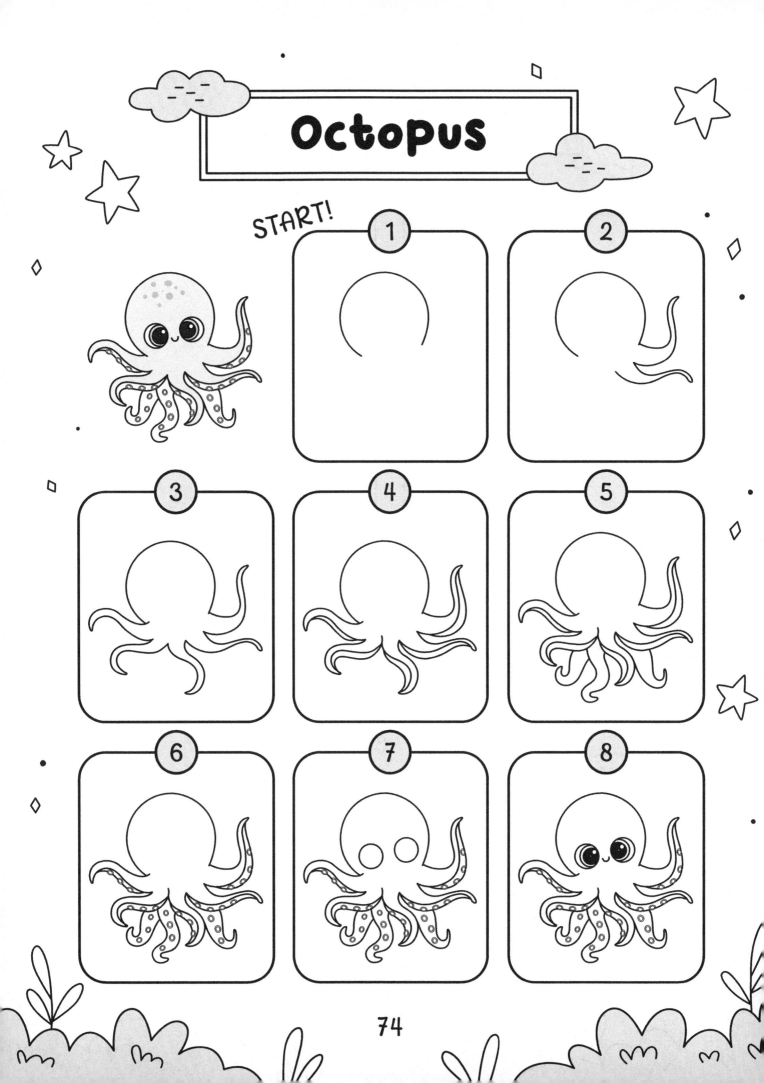

Octopuses have three hearts, and their blood is blue!

Practice Here

A B C D E F G H I J

1
2
3
4
5
6
7
8
9
10

A B C D E F G H I J

1
2
3
4
5
6
7
8
9
10

75

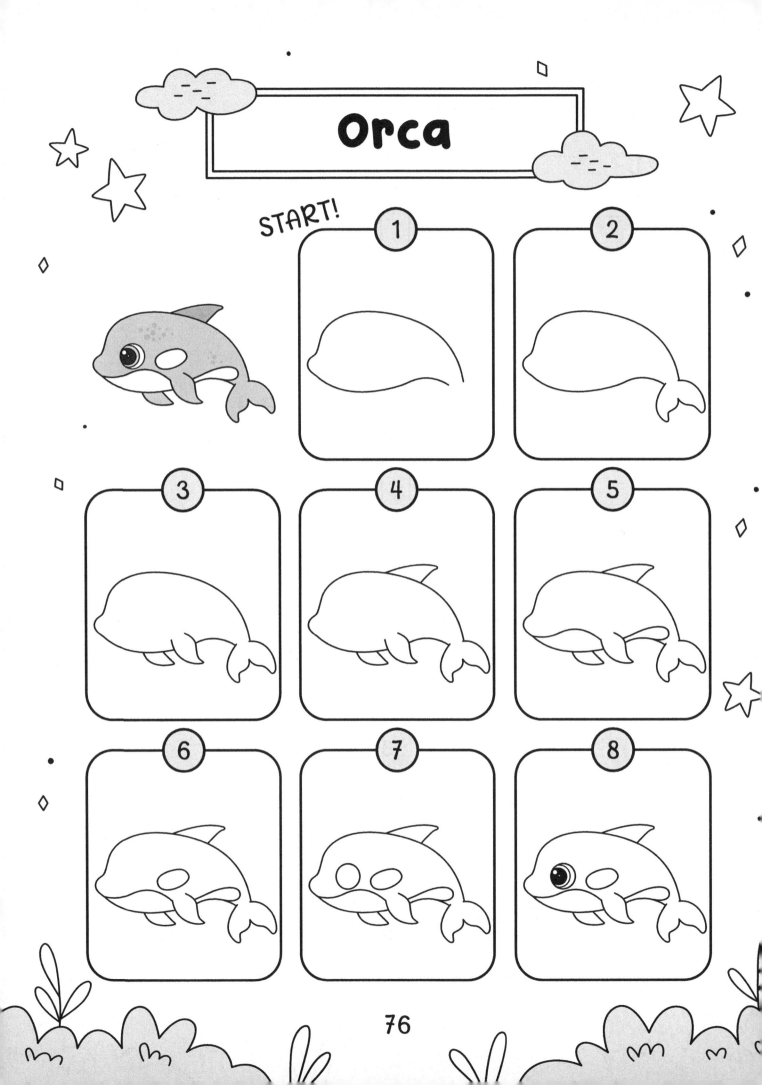

Orca

START!

1

2

3

4

5

6

7

8

Orcas are very social and live in groups called pods.

Practice Here

A B C D E F G H I J

1
2
3
4
5
6
7
8
9
10

A B C D E F G H I J

1
2
3
4
5
6
7
8
9
10

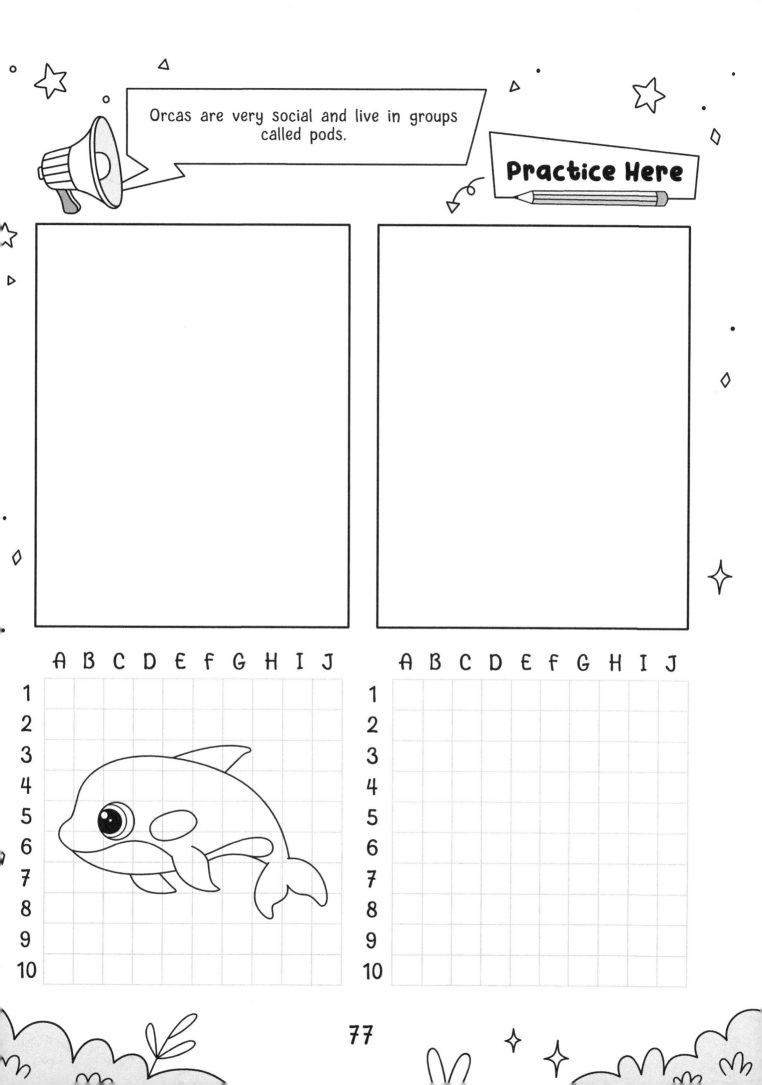

Otter

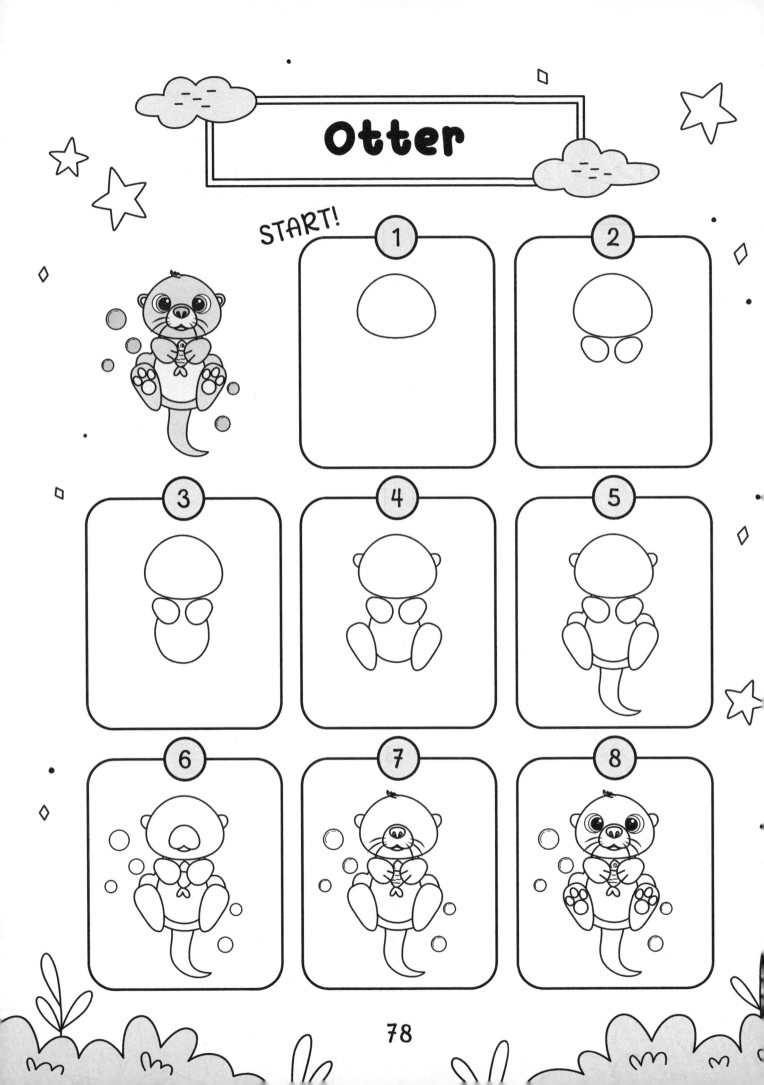

START!

Otters have a special pouch under their arms to store food while they swim.

Practice Here

A B C D E F G H I J

1
2
3
4
5
6
7
8
9
10

A B C D E F G H I J

1
2
3
4
5
6
7
8
9
10

Owl

START!

Owls can't move their eyes.

Practice Here

A B C D E F G H I J

1
2
3
4
5
6
7
8
9
10

A B C D E F G H I J

1
2
3
4
5
6
7
8
9
10

Panda

START!

The panda spends 14–16 hours a day eating bamboo.

Practice Here

A B C D E F G H I J

1
2
3
4
5
6
7
8
9
10

A B C D E F G H I J

1
2
3
4
5
6
7
8
9
10

Parrot

START!

They often have a good sense of humor and enjoy making their owners laugh.

Practice Here

A B C D E F G H I J

1
2
3
4
5
6
7
8
9
10

A B C D E F G H I J

1
2
3
4
5
6
7
8
9
10

Peacock

START!

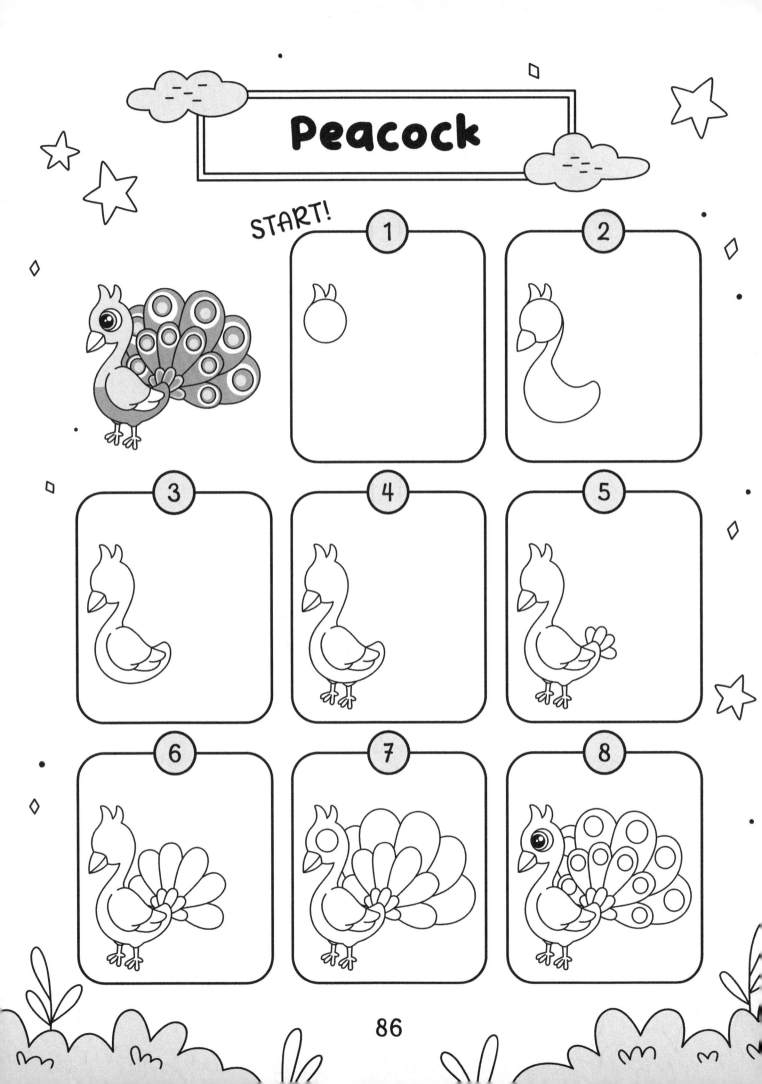

Peacock feathers are made up of tiny, individual "eyespots" that create dazzling patterns.

Practice Here

A B C D E F G H I J

1
2
3
4
5
6
7
8
9
10

A B C D E F G H I J

1
2
3
4
5
6
7
8
9
10

Penguin

START!

Penguins don't have any teeth at all.

A B C D E F G H I J

1
2
3
4
5
6
7
8
9
10

A B C D E F G H I J

1
2
3
4
5
6
7
8
9
10

Pufferfish

START!

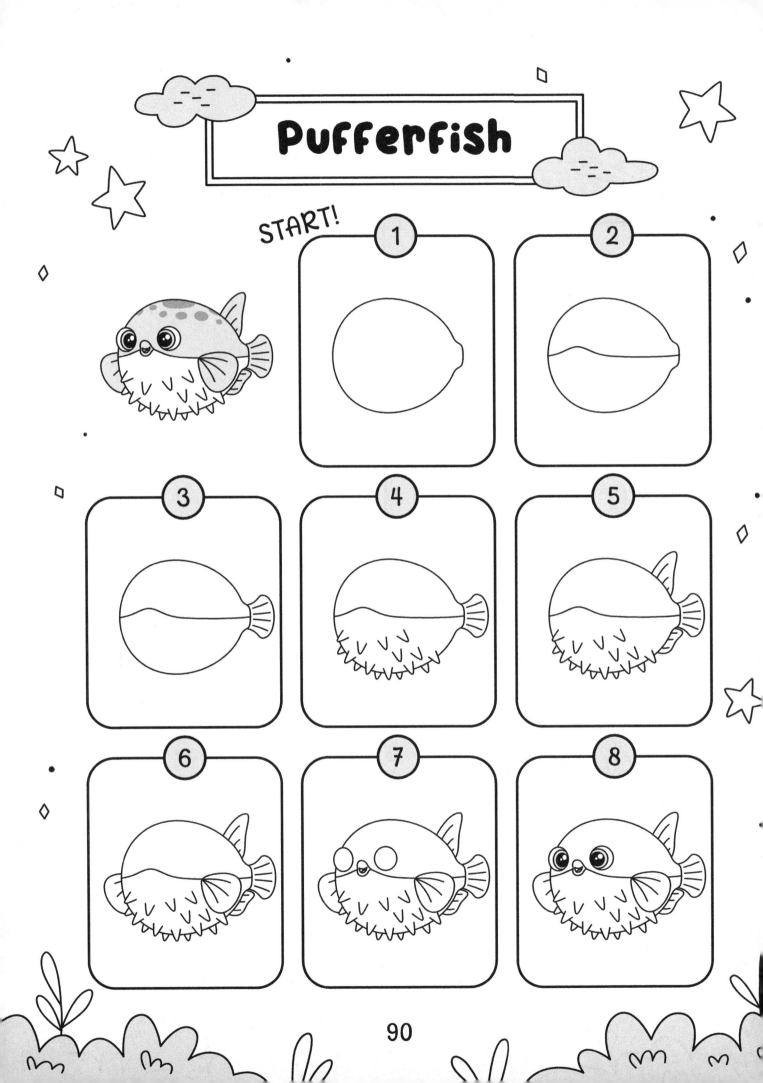

The more colorful the pufferfish is, the more poisonous it is.

Practice Here

A B C D E F G H I J

1
2
3
4
5
6
7
8
9
10

A B C D E F G H I J

1
2
3
4
5
6
7
8
9
10

Puffin

START!

1
2
3
4
5
6
7
8

They can hold up to 60 small fish in their beaks at once.

Practice Here

A B C D E F G H I J

1
2
3
4
5
6
7
8
9
10

A B C D E F G H I J

1
2
3
4
5
6
7
8
9
10

Raccoon

START!

1
2
3
4
5
6
7
8

94

Raccoons have a habit of washing their food in water before eating it.

Practice Here

```
   A  B  C  D  E  F  G  H  I  J
 1
 2
 3
 4
 5
 6
 7
 8
 9
10
```

```
   A  B  C  D  E  F  G  H  I  J
 1
 2
 3
 4
 5
 6
 7
 8
 9
10
```

Red Panda

START!

1 2 3 4 5 6 7 8

96

They have thick fur to keep them warm in cold mountain habitats.

Practice Here

A B C D E F G H I J

1
2
3
4
5
6
7
8
9
10

A B C D E F G H I J

1
2
3
4
5
6
7
8
9
10

Seahorse

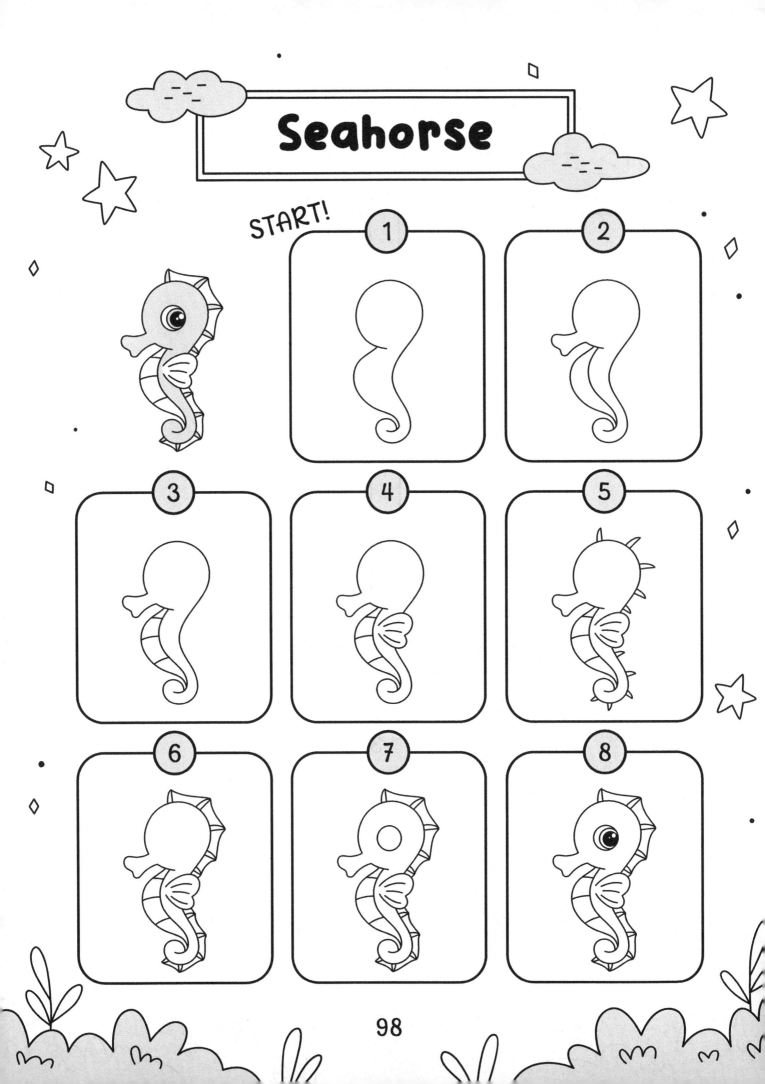

START!

Male seahorses carry and give birth to their babies.

Practice Here

A B C D E F G H I J

1
2
3
4
5
6
7
8
9
10

A B C D E F G H I J

1
2
3
4
5
6
7
8
9
10

Seal

START!

Seals can sleep underwater and surface for air without waking up.

Practice Here

A B C D E F G H I J

1
2
3
4
5
6
7
8
9
10

A B C D E F G H I J

1
2
3
4
5
6
7
8
9
10

Shark

START!

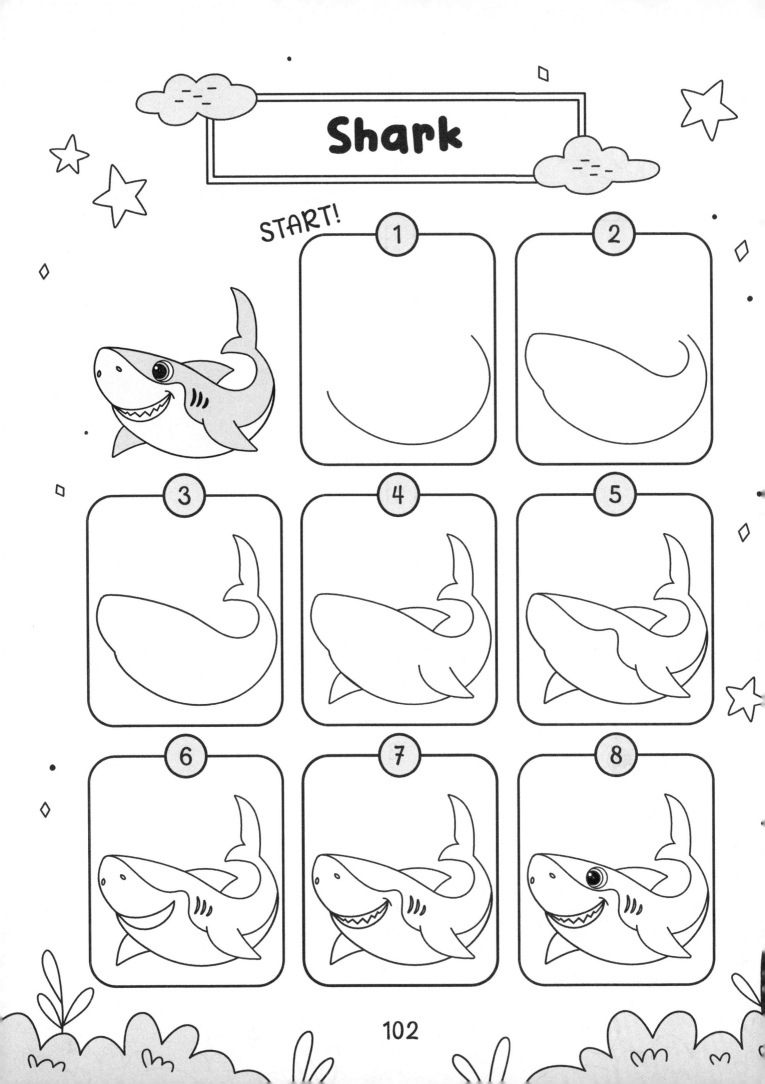

Sharks can only swim forward.

Practice Here

A B C D E F G H I J

1
2
3
4
5
6
7
8
9
10

A B C D E F G H I J

1
2
3
4
5
6
7
8
9
10

Sloth

START!

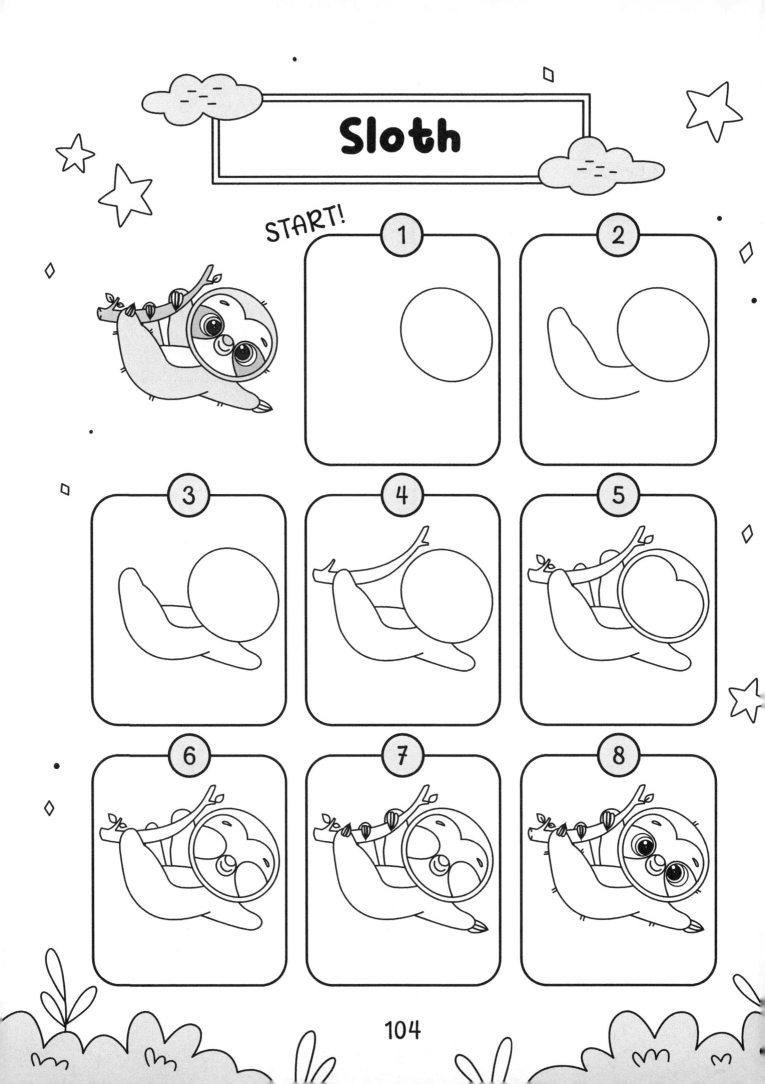

They only come down from trees once a week to go to the bathroom.

Practice Here

A B C D E F G H I J

1
2
3
4
5
6
7
8
9
10

A B C D E F G H I J

1
2
3
4
5
6
7
8
9
10

Snail

START!

1 2 3 4 5 6 7 8

A snail can sleep for three years in a row.

Practice Here

A B C D E F G H I J

1
2
3
4
5
6
7
8
9
10

A B C D E F G H I J

1
2
3
4
5
6
7
8
9
10

Snake

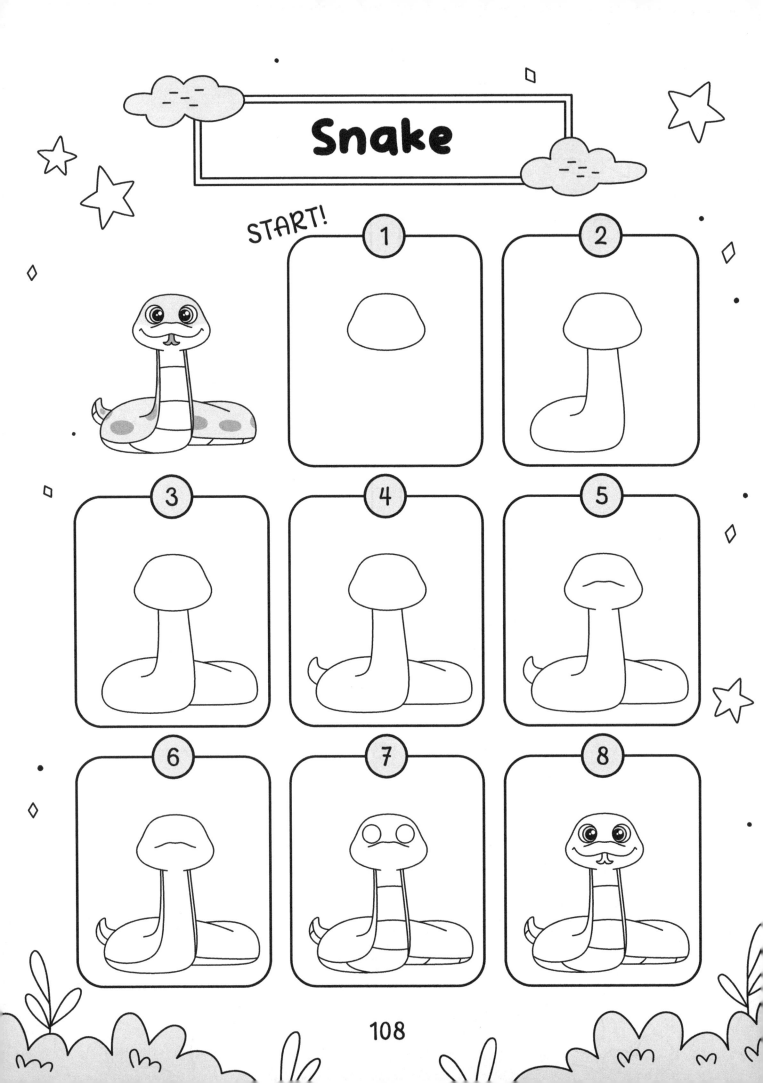

START!

1
2
3
4
5
6
7
8

Snakes shed their skin several times a year to allow for growth.

Practice Here

A B C D E F G H I J

1
2
3
4
5
6
7
8
9
10

A B C D E F G H I J

1
2
3
4
5
6
7
8
9
10

Spider

START!

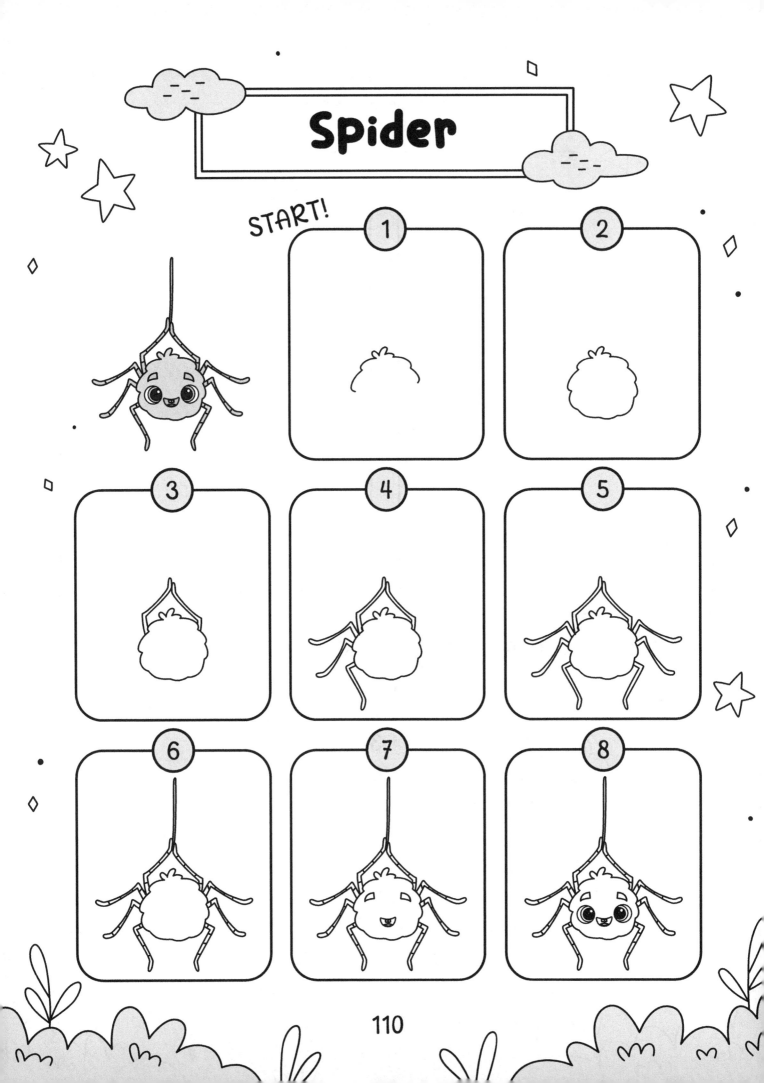

Some spiders can spin webs that are stronger than steel.

Practice Here

A B C D E F G H I J   A B C D E F G H I J

1   1
2   2
3   3
4   4
5   5
6   6
7   7
8   8
9   9
10   10

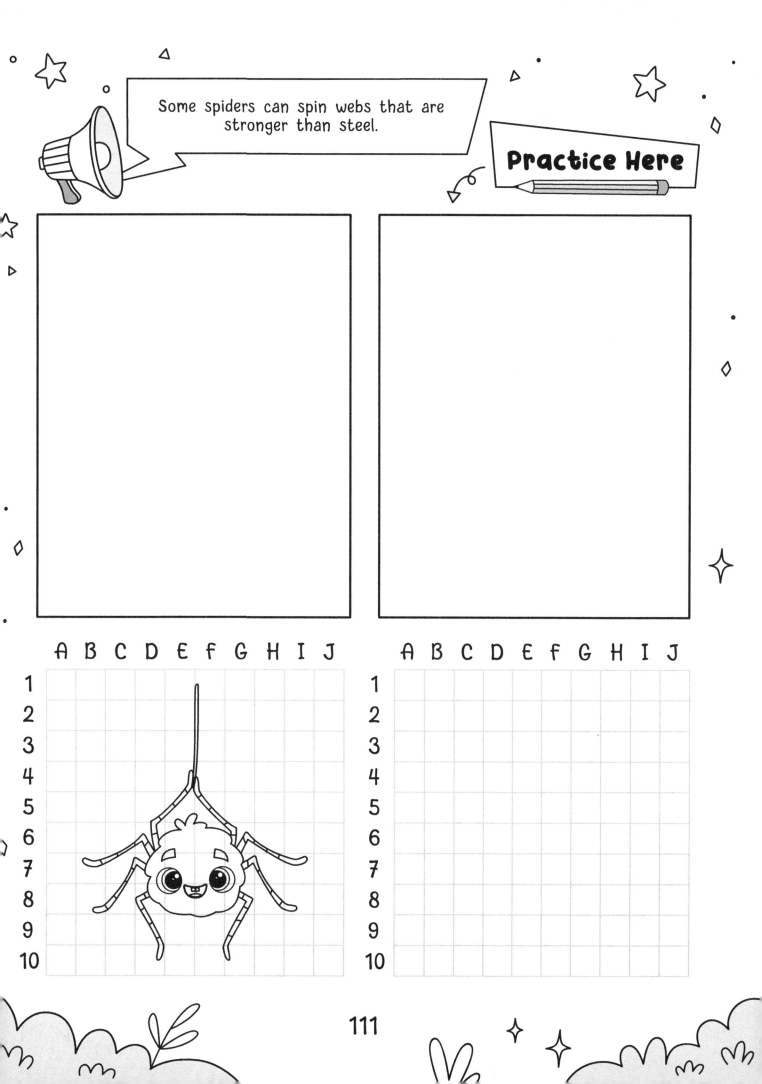

Squirrel

START!

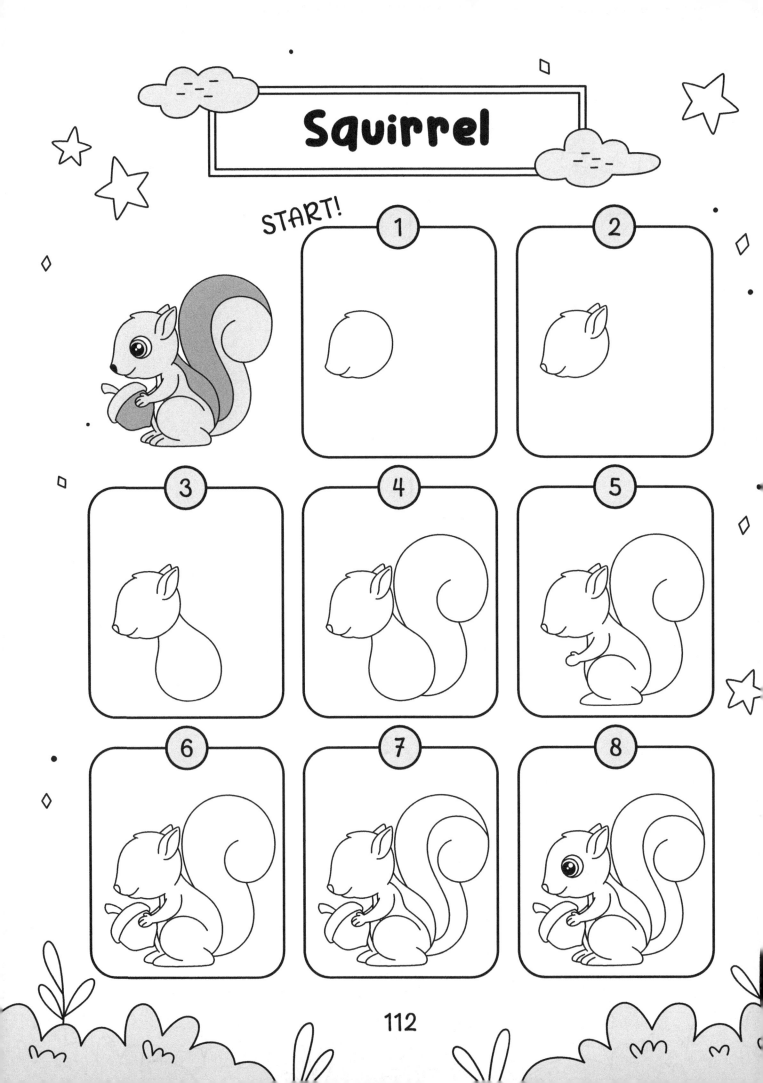

112

Squirrels can remember hundreds of hiding places for their food.

Practice Here

A B C D E F G H I J

1
2
3
4
5
6
7
8
9
10

A B C D E F G H I J

1
2
3
4
5
6
7
8
9
10

Stegosaurus

START!

1

2

3

4

5

6

7

8

Stegosaurus had a brain the size of a walnut but a large body.

Practice Here

A B C D E F G H I J

1
2
3
4
5
6
7
8
9
10

A B C D E F G H I J

1
2
3
4
5
6
7
8
9
10

Stingray

START!

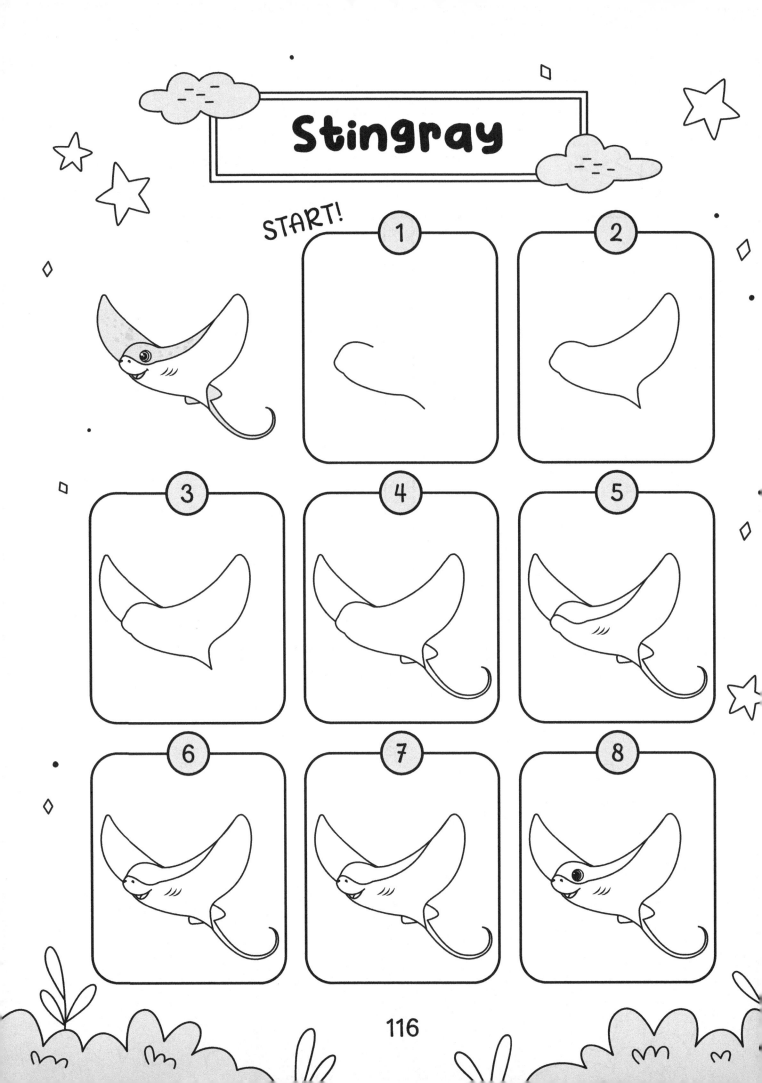

They use their tails to defend themselves by delivering painful stings.

Practice Here

A B C D E F G H I J

1
2
3
4
5
6
7
8
9
10

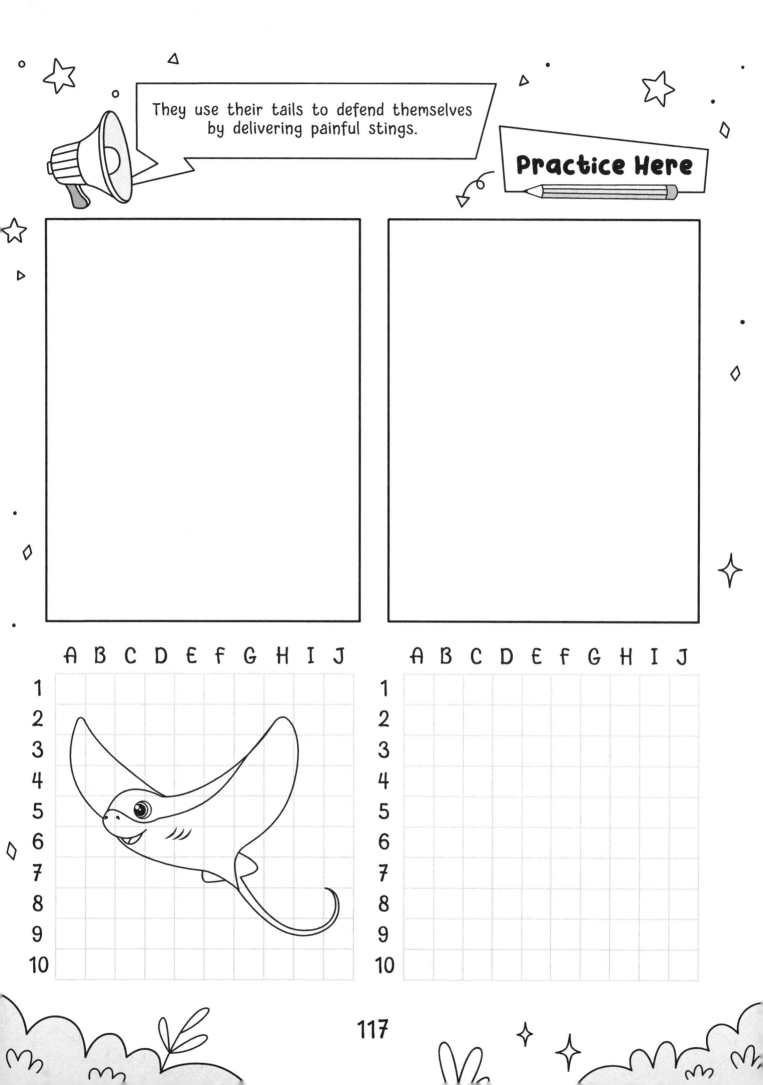

A B C D E F G H I J

1
2
3
4
5
6
7
8
9
10

Toucan

START!

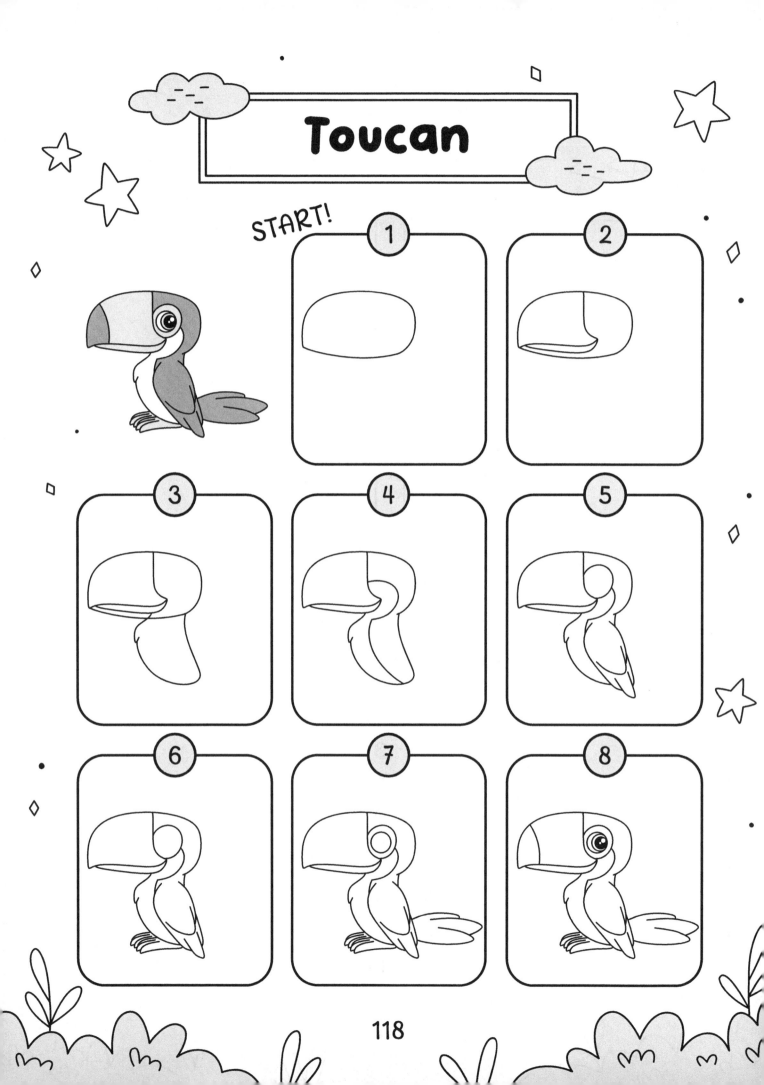

They are known for their loud, unique calls and songs.

Practice Here

A B C D E F G H I J

1
2
3
4
5
6
7
8
9
10

A B C D E F G H I J

1
2
3
4
5
6
7
8
9
10

Triceratops

START!

1
2
3
4
5
6
7
8

They had a bony frill on the back of their head for protection.

Practice Here

A B C D E F G H I J

1
2
3
4
5
6
7
8
9
10

A B C D E F G H I J

1
2
3
4
5
6
7
8
9
10

Turtle

START!

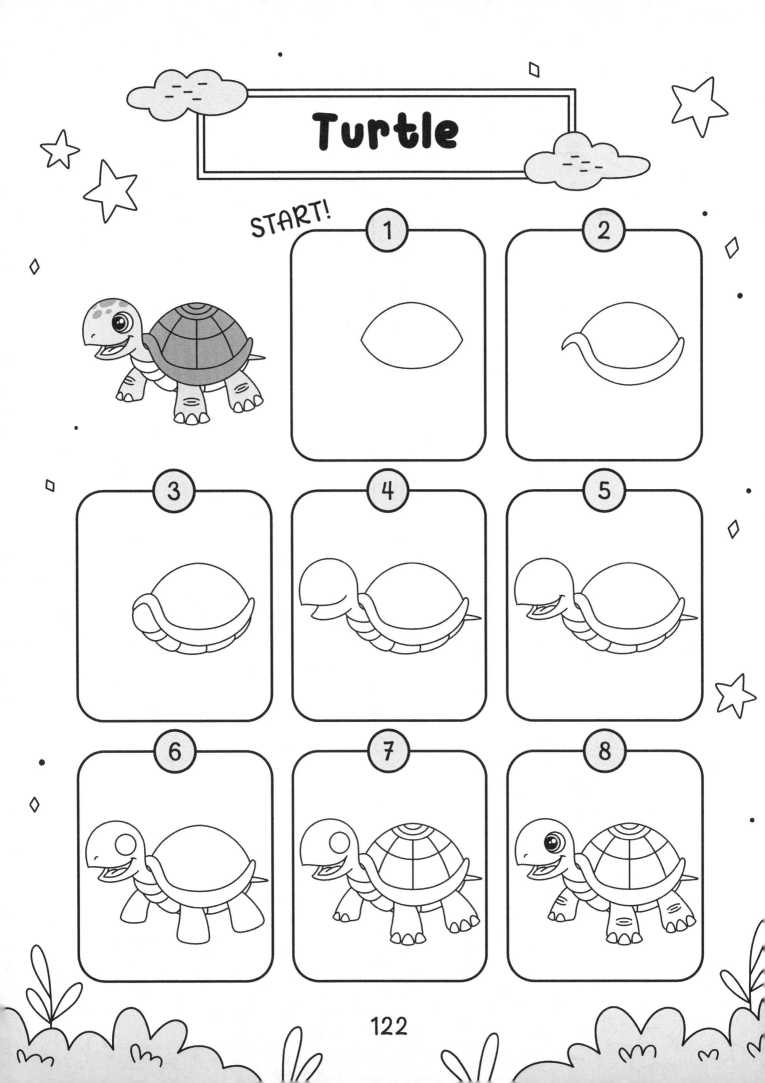

Some turtles can live for over 100 years!

Practice Here

A B C D E F G H I J

1
2
3
4
5
6
7
8
9
10

A B C D E F G H I J

1
2
3
4
5
6
7
8
9
10

123

Tyrannosaurus

START!

They were as long as a school bus and weighed as much as an elephant.

Practice Here

A B C D E F G H I J

1
2
3
4
5
6
7
8
9
10

A B C D E F G H I J

1
2
3
4
5
6
7
8
9
10

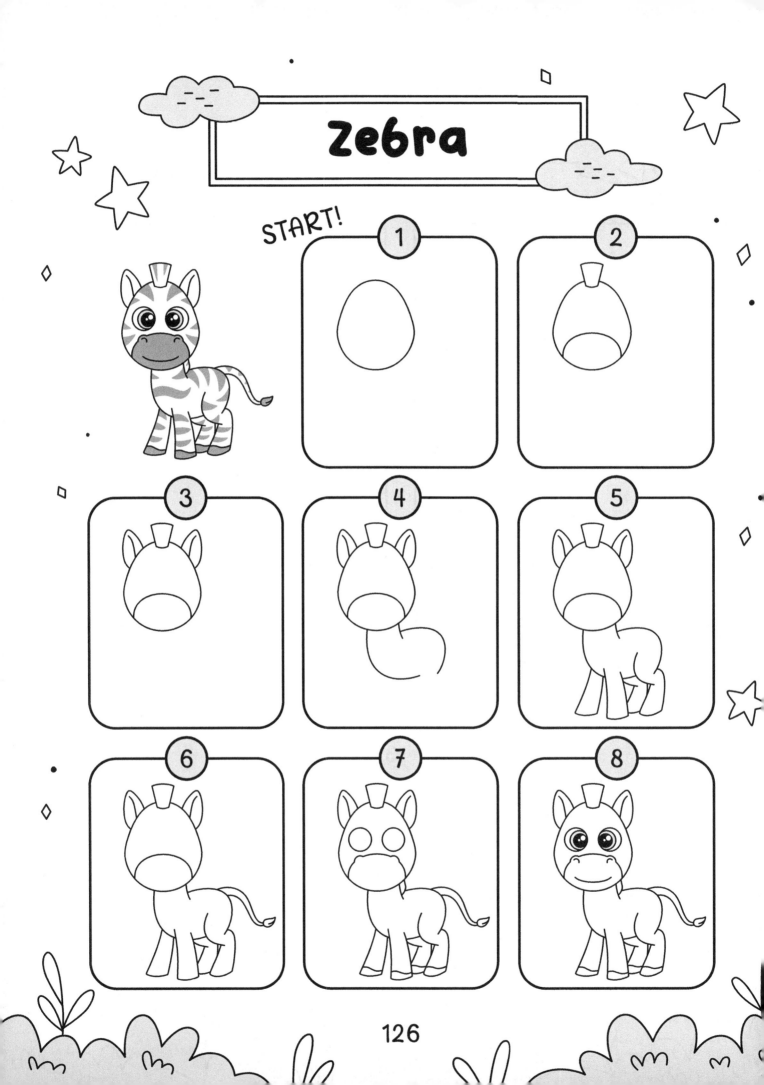

zebra

START!

1
2
3
4
5
6
7
8

126

A zebra's stripes are as unique as a human's fingerprints.

Practice Here

A B C D E F G H I J

1
2
3
4
5
6
7
8
9
10

A B C D E F G H I J

1
2
3
4
5
6
7
8
9
10

Made in the USA
Middletown, DE
01 October 2023

39895237R00071